MYSTERY OF THE ORDINARY

8 Statements Your Kids Need to Hear ... And Why!

Linc Taylor

Mystery of the Ordinary: 8 Statements Your Kids Need to Hear … And Why!

ISBN: 9781614841937

For my mom and dad—Bob and Beth

**They chose presence daily
and modeled the power of the
ordinary in family life.**

**For my wife, JoEllen,
and three daughters—
Grace, Joy Beth, and Lynna**

**Thanks for allowing me
to live out family with you.**

What an adventure!

Endorsements

"Since Solomon's writings, we have known that the heart—the inner person—determines all surface behavior. Sadly, the lost culture is beginning to figure that out. Those wanting to draw in our children now use algorithms, artificial intelligence, and subliminal media messages to capture children below the surface. That is why Linc Taylor's new book, *Mystery of the Ordinary*, is unique and thus valuable. Linc has provided believing parents with a practical plan for speaking truth to the eight most pivotal regions of their children's being below the surface. Because of the power of the Word and the Spirit, parents' voices will almost always prevail over the culture's counterfeit voices. I strongly encourage every believing parent to digest this book."

Richard Ross, PhD, Senior Professor of Student Ministry
at Southwestern Seminary in Fort Worth
RichardARoss.com

"In four decades of ministry to teenagers, I've met countless parents humbled by the challenge of parenting. Sadly, most end up hoping just to survive. What Linc offers parents is so much more. I have had the privilege to know and see Linc model these words as he and JoEllen have raised their own family. Thoughtful and practical, yet simple enough for any of us to apply. I hope your invitation to learn from his wisdom and experience leaves you encouraged and equipped for your parenting journey."

John Vicary
Former Executive VP for Young Life

"Linc Taylor's, *Mystery of the Ordinary: 8 Statements Your Kids Need to Hear ... And Why!* is a must read for parents looking for practical ways to connect their children to the gospel. Rather than a complicated new set of expectations, Linc encourages parents to embrace the ordinary aspects of life as opportunities to parent with purpose. Parents will find this book an enjoyable read that will produce a rich return on their investment."

Dr. Tate Cockrell
Professor of Counseling / Director of D.Min. Studies
Southeastern Baptist Theological Seminary

"On any journey, you need a trusted guide. For over 20 years I've watched Linc Taylor practice what he preaches in his marriage, his parenting, and in the ministries of our church. I've hiked more than a few trails with him as well! Now Linc is sharing his biblically-rooted, field-tested, and practically-driven wisdom with you. Pick up this guide and put it into practice one step at a time and you'll be amazed at the difference it makes in your everyday parenting for God's glory and your joy!"

Dr. Jay Strother
Senior Pastor, Brentwood Baptist Church

"These days, families come is all shapes and sizes. But the one thing that remains true is the importance of nurturing our often-delicate family relationships. Dr. Linc Taylor's book *Mystery of the Ordinary* is a must read for anyone looking to understand and even improve those significant relationships."

Gordon S. Kerr
CEO, Black River Entertainment

"Parenting can be the source of our biggest joys and challenges. My longtime friend, Linc Taylor does a masterful job of focusing in on what every child needs, wants, and prospers under from their parents. *Mystery of the Ordinary* provides the wisdom and tools we all need to be extraordinary parents. Enjoy the journey as you read."

Gregg Matte
Pastor of Houston's First Baptist Church

"God, prayer, love, acceptance, forgiveness, time … family. When you look in the mirror what do you see? Your children are paying attention. This book is an incredible reminder that as parents, we don't have to do it alone. As we strive to raise our children for His glory, the Lord is with us."

Angie Gentry
Widow of Troy Gentry of award-winning
country duo Montgomery Gentry

Table of Contents

Introduction

Years ago, I came home with a simple new children's toy for my kids. After making the room as dark as possible, we all excitedly sat down on the floor together, full of anticipation as I opened the box and prepared to flip the switch. We all gasped with delight as light shot through tiny holes, creating images of star constellations all over the room, and all over us. The small light in this box illuminated an ordinary room with extraordinary images. The backdrop of everyday walls and ceiling now captured and displayed new and transformed beams of light. A common, normal, and familiar place we had been in so many times came alive, transformed with a view that stirred in us a remarkable sense of wonder.

In a sense, I hope you begin to see a similar wonder and understanding of family! May your view of the common and ordinary spaces of family life gain new lenses and your sense of wonder toward family be reignited. We have an opportunity to intentionally lead and encourage our children in the most normal spaces of family life, which can have an eternal influence.

God's design of family is purposeful, and He invites us as parents to join Him on this great adventure. Family provides a setting for shared experiences where we showcase forgiveness, grace, restoration, community, and the gospel—right in the middle of our utter chaos, confusion, imperfect relationships, and misunderstood priorities.

I believe many of us find ourselves in one of four buckets that describe our current family life:

Scattered

You're just trying to keep it all together and not have everything fly off the handle. Time together around the dinner table, feeling like a full-time hired driver, and attempts at meaningful dialogue are sporadic and strewn all over the place like a debris field after a tornado has come through. Being overwhelmed is a constant. Know this—I see you!

Focused

You have intentional time with your family, occasionally a devotion occurs, car rides become places for healthy conversation, and everyone mostly acts as if they like each other. Vision and direction of family is mostly set and every now and then you recognize moments reflective of that vision. You feel pretty good about things right now, but you know there is always more to learn. I also had you in mind!

Fragmented

Some words and definitions of family that have been thrown your way include blended, broken, divorced, single-parent, or even shattered. You might find yourself at a crossroads of life that you never would have imagined. Hopefully, reconciliation and beauty are beginning to emerge as the hallmarks of your family, or maybe that narrative seems unattainable to you right now. Know this—the story is continuing to be written in your home and God's plan and purpose can absolutely be on full display. You were often on my mind when I wrote this book. I see you!

Dissatisfied

Maybe you've said this in the last week or so… "there has to be more to all this!" You are motivated to do something different, but you don't know what to do. You are not sure of the bigger purpose of family, so you just keep doing the same thing. Maybe you don't think you're spiritual enough, you weren't raised in a healthy home, or you simply feel inadequate, so you're stuck in a sense of hopelessness. Maybe you are believing some lies. Please know—I had you in mind when I wrote this book!

Maybe you're a grandparent, teacher, or minister, or you work with children in various settings. I believe the principles and encouragements are easily contextualized into your area of influence.

What This Isn't…

- A hidden recipe or strategy to successful parenting or a failsafe way to impress truths on your kids
- An exhaustive list of all truths that need to be spoken to your kids
- An exhaustive list of all the deeper needs your kids have
- A Bible study—although it is birthed out of and based on truths from God's Word
- The end-all family-ministry approach. Although foundational, it's just one thread of a much larger discussion to continue as you build intentionality and spiritually lead your kids.

What This Is…

- An exploration of powerful opportunities for parents to be intentional in impacting their children, most often in the midst of the everyday and ordinary of family life
- An attempt to help the reader understand the larger background shaping the impact of a pragmatic approach of parenting undergirded by truths from Scripture
- Tangible ways to speak words of hope and identity into your kids
- An effort to create an awareness of the below-the-surface needs our kids have, the role parents can play in helping to meet those needs—and knowing the world offers counterfeit responses to all these needs.

My prayer for you is laser-focused! May you become encouraged and refreshed in how you view the role and opportunity of leading and influencing your child. As you turn the pages, I pray you are moved to pause and intentionally deliberate. Maybe you just sit with the Lord and journal for a while. I also pray for those times you feel you are on a roller coaster of emotions because you encounter new or resurfaced ideas that disturb the status quo of your family life. Lean into those stirrings that take place in your heart—even in the areas you find overwhelming or a bit too personal. We are all in this together!

I'm looking forward to your journey as you view your family in a new and fresh way. May you recognize anew the opportunity of parenting as you fashion the ordinary hum of life with your kids and move it toward extraordinary impact.

C'mon!

Linc Taylor

MYSTERY OF THE ORDINARY:

8 Statements Your Kids Need to Hear...And Why!

Chapter 1

The Ordinary and Extraordinary

The fireplace crackled with life in an almost empty rustic lobby. I found myself sitting in a lodge staring at a laptop computer screen outside of Santa Fe, New Mexico on my first sabbatical. After a day of hiking and being surrounded by incredible views, I now was settling in to try to answer the things that were swirling in my mind. Wrestling is the better term to use as I attempted to find handles for the challenge of inspiring parents for ordinary days.

Great insights were being produced by ministries and churches to help parents navigate the reality of family. We were celebrating milestones, scripting out devotions, and offering training. But the issue that had me grappling the most was, how do we equip parents for the other 95 percent of the time? What about preparing the heart of a parent for impactful moments in the margins of life where there was no script?

Another key element demanding to be addressed was, every family dynamic is unique. Every home's makeup, personality, and rhythm of life is different. Not every parent is in the same place spiritually or in how they have been discipled. If a script is laid out, we assume so much. I was convicted that many families were being left out of the equation when strategies were being developed. Many accomplished, confident people can't see themselves discipling their kids. I was compelled to encourage them to get there.

The challenge kept growing to create some clear paths of purposeful family that parents from all family dynamics could begin to see themselves traveling. Could we give them a modest step to take, then encourage another one, and before long they find themselves being intentional in the rhythms of their unique family dynamic? As I sat there, specific questions began to come to mind that could lead toward encouraging and reassuring parents they can see real progress.

Could shepherding ordinary moments lead toward extraordinary influence?

- Could shepherding ordinary moments lead toward extra-ordinary influence?
- What are some ingredients of true parental influence?
- What things affect the quality of the relationship between a parent and a child?
- What happens when we aren't perfect, and we just blow it in a parenting decision?
- What deep hidden needs are churning in the heart of a child that parents need to know?
- Does it really matter when parents speak encouraging words to a child who acts like they don't care?
- While we can't design a formula that has an exact outcome, what if parents could really envision the impact of impressing God's Word on the hearts of their kids in the real everyday life of family?

Then my mind went straight to all the obstacles that stop many parents' determination to lead their family purposefully. I had personally heard many through the years in ministry. Let's name the obstacles, let parents know they aren't alone, and move forward together, even with all the uncertainty that comes with it, because we are trusting a big God to move in these seemingly big obstacles we can't see past. Obstacles can make things challenging, but they don't have to prevent us from the victory of progress.

Here are a few:

- It's awkward when I try to lead.
- I didn't grow up in a home where this was modeled.
- I feel so inadequate.
- My kids are too old to begin.
- I have no idea where to start.
- And on and on…

The wrestling that began in earnest that night in a New Mexico lodge has continued to swirl in my mind and heart. But a path forward has also become clearer. My experiences in ministry for over 35 years, being a dad of three daughters, academic research as I pursued my Master's and D.Min. degrees, and thousands of in-depth conversations over the years with students, parents, and ministry leaders all helped shape my convictions.

So, I offer you these thoughts on some practical next steps and with the hope you will gain a larger perspective of family. I hope you consider how some of the principles apply in your family. Mine is just one voice in a much larger conversation into being and doing family intentionally, and I pray you come away inspired.

When to Put the Brush Down

My wife is an aspiring artist who loves to draw and paint. She finds it difficult to decide when to put the brush away and declare the work done. The more she looks over the painting, the more she sees spaces paint could be added. But so often beauty is most captivating when something is left to the imagination. In parenting and family, so much more could be added and scripted, but keeping a sharpened focus on purpose and intentionality in the ordinary leaves us some breathing room as parents. Parents really can worry less about the details and comparison pressures and lean confidently into purpose and the joy of being family.

I pray this resource encourages you in the chaotic privilege of passing faith to the next generation! You are not alone in your struggles and feeling insufficient as you parent. I hope God does something remarkable as you read.

Get a Journal

Get a journal you could utilize throughout this book. There will be many opportunities to take notes, answer questions, or write down prompts you might have that could be related to intentionality in your family.

Ordinary and Extraordinary Moments

Who doesn't love experiencing or witnessing extraordinary events? I love the wonder of astonishing times that rarely happen and when they do, cause us to sit in silence because words just won't capture what is unfolding. These moments are outside the norm of our daily lives. Considered special, unique, or astonishing—they strike deep chords in us and cause an awareness of our place in the world or realization that life is more than what we had understood. Here are a few of those moments for me:

- Standing at the altar with my brand-new bride after saying our vows
- Being in the delivery room and witnessing the birth of our children
- Walking out to the viewpoint at Glacier Point in Yosemite National Park
- My baptism in my home church
- Sitting in our family room and receiving the call from my brother that my dad had just died and realizing his faith is now sight
- After perilous climbing, resting on the top of Angels Landing in Zion National Park
- Kneeling with my wife in what many consider to be the actual empty tomb in Jerusalem
- Leading a person through the Scriptures, and they give their life to Christ right there

I'm sure you can name your moments, too. Those moments when all the big and small things in your life simply pause and time appears to stand still. Why are these extraordinary moments so powerful to us? What is the common theme when we experience these times that cause us to pause?

Some of those feelings can be captured this way.

- We gain perspective and outlook in life. We realize what is truly important.

- We are awed by the moment and are challenged to comprehend what we are experiencing.
- We are quickly ushered to a view that allows us to see things we could not see otherwise.
- We sit or stand in silence, because words fall so short to capture the moment.

Larger-than-life settings can jolt us to see things differently. They are special, needed, and are truly extraordinary. This is especially true in our relationship with God and each other. I'm a big fan of experiencing catalytic moments and being awakened from a slumber that I might find myself in because I am either consumed by the daily hum around me or I've become complacent with my own comforts of life. In the reality of family, we can strategically place our individual family members into moments that cause them to wake up and see things differently.

These moments are like seeing mountains from above 10,000 feet where unobstructed views of the surrounding beauty astound us. Perception changes and we see everything clearer. But here's the reality; we don't live in those out of ordinary times consistently in the daily rhythms of our lives. They are usually shorter moments in time and generally don't last long. Oxygen levels are lower and not much grows above those heights. Being in the valley and plains of life is where the ordinary happens, and the place where the deeper work of life change and impact can occur.

The Mystery of the Ordinary

I'm just as big a fan of recognizing the opportunity of everyday moments in life, especially in relating within family. Yes, experience the mountain top and catch a glimpse of the amazement but make the effort to live with intention in the ordinary. Found in the strength of relationships we have with our kids and the use of our words and conversations, these are the places where opportunities are wide open to have ongoing influence. These moments might not be considered extraordinary as they happen, but the impression that is slowly occurring in the hearts of our kids can be life altering.

As parents, and even a society, we see the highlights and Instagram moments where the formation that happened off the radar shows itself—like the important work in framing a new house or building. The frame that will soon enough be hidden from view with a veneer exterior gives shape to the structure that everyone notices. Although the framing that is done might seem unimpressive and not seen again after the brick and siding are put on, it is incredibly vital. While it's pure joy to do life as a family, the slow work of ongoing conversations and building a healthy relationship with your kids can appear unimpressive in making a mark on their lives. But it's the ordinary days where formation happens, those days that we wouldn't necessarily consider writing about even in our journal.

Found in the strength of relationships we have with our kids and the use of our words and conversations, these are the places where opportunities are wide open to have ongoing influence.

I think of the unwritten words that Paul said about Timothy's mother and grandmother. "I recall your sincere faith that first lived in your grandmother Lois and in your mother Eunice and now, I am convinced, is in you also" (2 Timothy 1:5).

These two pillars in Timothy's life obviously left an impression of the Lord on his life. But when Paul referenced faith that "lived in your grandmother…and mother," we don't really think of an extraordinary moment that caused Timothy's life to forever change. Paul left us to consider the fact that these two women showcased a love for the Lord in the everyday. They most likely sat down with him and went through the law and the prophets and even had him memorize passages. They also impacted him with the ordinary and repeated rhythms of their home life, the choices they made, the words they spoke, and the ways they spent their money.

The challenge is to become a family, uniquely created and assembled by God, that bravely prioritizes the things of God wholistically and threads biblical truths into the fabric of the ordinary moments in our homes.

Maybe the impact came through the first words they said to him each morning or the closing conversation they had each night. Timothy may have noticed in the fields when they gathered grain together, or through the laughter they shared around the campfire at night. We don't have details about the everyday vignettes where formation happened, but we know that formation did occur, evident in Timothy's life that was first "lived" in these two influential women in the mystery of the ordinary.

No exact script to follow exists for the ordinary. It's an awareness of the opportunity of family that is bigger than you realize. It's being the family you are and pivoting the intentionality while wearing kingdom lenses. Kingdom perception grants us the benefit of envisioning what the important elements of family can be as we allow God to transform our hearts into His character. Although some of us might need to alter our rhythms of family life and make hard turns, I don't think God is asking you to be a family you wouldn't recognize, necessarily. The challenge is to become a family, uniquely created and assembled by God, that bravely prioritizes the things of God wholistically and threads biblical truths into the fabric of the ordinary moments in our homes. The verbal cadence of your home will have a familiar God-given melody based on personalities and other factors, with kingdom harmonies mingled throughout with intention to create a richer composition that enhances each of the ordinary spaces of your family life.

Setting the Level

We were having one of the biggest fights in our marriage up to that point. It didn't have to do with one of the biggies like money, one of us not feeling loved, or some other unmet expectation. I'm not sure which one of us decided we needed to hang vertical striped wallpaper at the end of a long day, but that became the backdrop of this epic, yet ridiculous, dispute. (Since I am the one writing this, we will say it was JoEllen's idea.) We had been married about five years and were continuing to work and redecorate our older house. Thinking we could complete this job quickly one evening after our young daughters went to sleep, we soon discovered we were in for an ordeal big enough to end up in a book one day.

We didn't yet know this fact, but walls aren't necessarily straight in older homes. We did learn it quickly when we put up a level for the wallpaper with stripes needing to be straight. We decided to start in the corner on the left and realized that although the stripes were straight next to the wall in the corner, it still seemed off. Even going to the other corner, same conclusion—that wall wasn't straight either. Working with your spouse to make wallpaper with large vertical stripes look right with both side walls crooked can test any marriage. But we survived that night and got the wallpaper up by starting in the middle. Tall bookshelves and a large plant helped to hide the imperfections in the corners. We still remember just about every detail of that fun evening. It's wild that it took putting up a level for us to realize the situation we'd been living in all along.

There were two issues we had to push through that night.

- Each of our reactions when we discovered the walls weren't straight—We had been in that home for well over two years and had no idea that the walls in our most used room were so crooked.
- Now what? Where and how do we begin to make it all work? We weren't initially on the same page about how to proceed.

What do you do when you discover that walls aren't completely straight?

Chapter 2

Where Are We Now?

Consider the simple list of eight statements I am encouraging you to emphasize with your kids. These powerful words can speak truth and encouragement into the minds and hearts of your family when they become themes in your household.

"I'm so glad you're in our family!"

"I'm praying for you today!"

"I believe in you!"

"True life is found in Christ!"

"I've got your back!"

"I forgive you!"

"I love you!"

"Join me in reaching people with the Gospel!"

Before we can truly understand the impact of these statements, we need to take a sincere look at where we are as families and plow the ground of our own hearts to turn over reasons we don't always naturally speak biblical life and hope at home. We also need to explore the power of these statements and the incredible privilege we have to impact our children with gospel truths in the ordinary of family.

Come with me on a journey. I invite you to observe your family dynamic from a different or possibly new perspective. You might say we are going to put up a level next to the walls of your family life. It's a step back from the day-to-day grind of trying to "do" family life and take a fresh look or check-up on how things are playing out. I think we as parents would do well to pause more often, take the time to gauge our family reality and come to an honest assessment of how we're doing in relationships and direction of family life or purpose. Many times, we are just responding to the immediate obligations. We are often controlled by or compelled to meet the impulses of the pressing matters that are right before us.

I think we as parents would do well to pause more often, take the time to gauge our family reality and come to an honest assessment of how we're doing in relationships and direction of family life or purpose.

We're all just trying to make it through this week's Monday schedule, Wednesday's homework project, or figuring out how we're going to make it to all the games our kids are a part of this weekend. And yes, next week's schedule might look even crazier. Many times, in my own home when our kids were younger, I remember often just trying to solve the immediate problem of getting everyone ready for school, church, an athletic event, a party, a practice, homework, or making sure our kids have matching shoes on (or have shoes on at all!) and not even having time to think about the bigger picture of why we're making the decisions we're making.

- What's driving us?
- Why do we "do" family like this?
- Are we doing family correctly?

- Are our kids thriving?
- Who decided this is the best way?
- What do I not know about my kids that I need to?
- What does God say about family?
- Am I just responding to what I think the culture around me expects of me as a parent? Where are we going as a family?
- Is there a pinnacle of family life, and if so, how do I know I've arrived?
- Do I even agree with the pace of our family life?

The questions go on and on.

Or maybe some of us have not even had time to think there is a bigger picture and meaning of family. I think we can all agree most of us are often in survival mode, and that's all we think we have time for. Do we stop and see if God has something to say about it all? What are the big rocks to the design of family? Is there truly a plan for the family that I might be missing? What should I really be doing as a parent? We often find ourselves not being sure in knowing steps to take to see the bigger picture. And if we did make the time to think about the big picture, we might find ourselves overwhelmed with the prospect of being intentional in our parenting and feeling completely unprepared to know what to do or find time to do it.

A Check-up on the Reality of Family Life

Here's what I invite you to do. Take a deep breath, let it out slowly, and pause for just a moment. If I were to ask you a simple question—How's your family doing? or How is life as a parent?—how would you answer it? I think most of us would give a default answer with a "you know, busy but doing fine." It's easier to respond, "doing fine," because we can keep doing what we're doing and not have to deal with the harder things. We all do it—dismiss, deflect, and move on! But for the sake, design, and hope of this book you're holding in your hands, that answer is not quite good enough, nor is it likely completely honest. I will take you along on a deeper dive into that question and do that by placing you into some common scenarios or situations with your family and kids.

You will be guided to take a Likert Scale assessment in how you view your family dynamics and relationship with your children in your home. The purpose of the assessment is to simply bring to the surface some observations on how your family might currently relate to each other, the content of conversations, and the overall health among family members. I hope it prepares your heart and mind to be ready to be challenged and encouraged with the content of later chapters. The more honest we can be with how things really are, the better we can move forward with more intentionality.

Be assured, the results won't be turned over to a governing board and potentially ding you on your parenting skills. This assessment is simply for you (and perhaps your spouse), to utilize and see things in a fresh way, taking fresh notice of some possible realities of your family.

Directions:

1. Work through each sentence one at a time before going to the next one.
2. Read each sentence, pause, and read it again. Maybe two or three times.
3. This is a Likert Scale—so you will circle (or answer in a separate journal) the number that most closely aligns with your assessment representing the current reality of your

home. Answer 1 if you Strongly Disagree; 5 if you Strongly Agree with the sentence related to how you parent or your family culture.

Here are the guidelines:

1. Take your time and be honest with yourself when you answer.
2. Don't answer with aspirational outlooks, answer with how things are currently.
3. If you assess your family is doing well in every area, then fantastic! But don't stop!
4. If you find yourself seeing ways you want to pivot in many of the situations of your home, hold on! Please release any temptation to feel fearful, guilty, remorseful, or overwhelmed. We simply want you to know where you are so you can take the next step forward.
5. If needed, adjust or reframe some of the sentences to match the current age of your kids.
6. Stop and pray right now! Pray that you can be as honest and reflective as possible.

Personal Family Assessment

Directions: 1 is *Strongly Disagree*, 5 is *Strongly Agree*.

1. My children come to me to seek wisdom, insight, or comfort.

   1 2 3 4 5

2. My children would say I make myself available for opportunities in which they can come to me and talk about issues they are going through.

   1 2 3 4 5

3. I celebrate and acknowledge to my children how proud I am of them apart from school grades, athletic awards, accomplishments, etc., (other than "performance" times).

   1 2 3 4 5

4. I know and appreciate the personality and disposition of my child.

   1 2 3 4 5

5. I put effort into creating times for our immediate family to be together and don't just wait for those moments to happen by chance.

   1 2 3 4 5

6. I know the two to three primary emotional and spiritual threats or vulnerabilities that my children are dealing with currently. (This could be peers, lies they tell themselves, temptations they are susceptible to, etc.)

   1 2 3 4 5

7. I can clearly state God's design for family.

   1 2 3 4 5

8. I verbally tell my kids that I am sorry for a mistake I have made.

   1 2 3 4 5

9. I forgive my kids when they disobey or embarrass me.

   1 2 3 4 5

10. I personally have shared a clear presentation of the gospel with my children.

   1 2 3 4 5

11. My kids know that I believe in them, no matter how young or old they are.

   1 2 3 4 5

12. Our family is characterized by circling up to pray together at places and times other than the dinner table.

   1 2 3 4 5

13. I ask my kids to go with me to serve others or to share the gospel with someone.

1 2 3 4 5

14. I talk with each of my kids one-on-one in a meaningful conversation, even though it might be short, at least once a day.

1 2 3 4 5

15. I seek to restore with my kids after I discipline them.

1 2 3 4 5

16. The relational atmosphere in our home is one of respect and love.

1 2 3 4 5

17. I feel inadequate to lead my kids spiritually and talk to them about biblical truths.

1 2 3 4 5

18. If I'm being honest, I would say I let the church do most, if not all, of the spiritual training of my children.

1 2 3 4 5

19. I deliberately create shared experiences for our family to be together and to build memories.

1 2 3 4 5

20. I tell each of my kids that I am proud of them when I see them making wise choices.

1 2 3 4 5

21. I still reach for my children to show affection—either physically or verbally—even when they act like they don't care.

1 2 3 4 5

22. My children know I will be in their corner when tough times come or when they feel alone.

1 2 3 4 5

23. I have told my kids "I love you" within the last week.

1 2 3 4 5

24. What I believe about the Lord is seen and lived out as a value in front of my kids through the choices I make.

1 2 3 4 5

25. I already have a trajectory set for my kids' lives—athletics, school, job, career, lifestyle—that I expect them to follow.

1 2 3 4 5

26. I'm too busy building a career and lifestyle to find time to intentionally lead my kids spiritually.

1 2 3 4 5

27. I find myself wanting to relive my youthful years through my kids' experiences.

1 2 3 4 5

28. I make time in my schedule to intentionally talk with my kids about biblical truths and what I'm learning from the Lord.

1 2 3 4 5

29. I seek to cultivate mission opportunities for our family other than what the church already offers.

1 2 3 4 5

30. I believe my life is too much of a mess to lead my kids spiritually.

1 2 3 4 5

After the Assessment

Here are two issues you might need to push through, like we did when we sat there in our living room realizing we had crooked living room walls.

- You may experience several responses when you discover the "walls" of your family might not be straight in areas that you thought were right on target. No need to feel guilt, shame, or being overwhelmed.
- Now what? Where and how do we begin to make it all work as a family moving forward? My hope is to assist and encourage you in taking some next steps in these moments.

As you were challenged to reflect and think through your family life, I pray it was insightful in some ways. Maybe this exercise brought to the surface at least a hint of the realities of your current family dynamics. Believe me, when I was developing these sentences and areas to evaluate, I was confronted with our own family dynamics when my kids were young, and I continue to reflect on our current relationships even though my daughters are grown and married. Whether we choose to gloss over our responses or not, we are challenged internally. For me, these single words captured some of my responses as I worked through each of the situations: adjust, focus, ooh, reset, naivety, ouch, yes, and determine. Maybe those were some words that could define your thoughts.

Possibly you are realizing some inner dissatisfaction regarding how your family is currently playing out, excitement for change, or a desire to have your kid's deeper needs met. Maybe you are discovering a desperate cry for help within, or an eagerness to know more about how Scripture is even brought into the everyday. Perhaps you sense something is missing in your ordinary homelife. Every family has areas to focus on anew, a need to move forward—and room to do so. The desire to make changes starts with realizing the need to do so. Be encouraged! We can release the pressure toward perfection and instead press into grace in the process.

Thoughts on Next Steps

1. Journal. Write down some of your thoughts
    a. **Pause**—pray, sit, and be still for a few moments.
    b. **Reflect** on some of the sentences where you responded "Strongly Agree" or in the "Strongly Disagree" area. What did you learn?

   c. **Listen** to what God might be revealing to you about yourself and your family.

2. Write down what you might already be prompted to do or think differently. Be ready throughout the book to journal when prompted.
3. Have coffee with your spouse or a trusted friend and go over the Assessment. You can challenge them to take it and then you discuss it together.
4. Pray. Feel free to use the following prayer as a guide or write your own.

Hands Open, Hands Up

(A Prayer of Lament and Worship for Parents by JoEllen Taylor)

I grieve, Father!
The swift prison of time,
The limited capacity of my mind to remember every expression and conversation,
The pain of rejection I feel when my kids choose others' leading,
Missed opportunities and misunderstandings.

I fear, Father!
The uncertainty of the future my children embrace,
The empty spaces and quiet at home,
The search for significance in the next season,
Costs of my sin to my heart, mind, and marriage.

I need, Father!
Identity solid in You and Your work and will,
Freedom in knowing You love them more,
Wise releasing of managing and scripting,
Courage to let them...learn to trust You.

But you, O Lord,
Hearer of my heart cries,
Merciful tender of my grazing heart,
Knitter of our being,
Tender Shepherd to me and to the children You placed here,

You beckon me to your side.
There is room to breathe,
To linger unhurried with You,
To be, and to be healed.
Help me trust, and even more, to entrust!

I see, Father!
You are working, loving, leading in the mystery of the ordinary.
I surrender all!
Hands open, hands up,
Help me guide them daily to views of Your glory!

Chapter 3

The Unique, God-Given Design of Family

Our clear guiding biblical challenge as we step into the role of parenthood comes from the truths found in Deuteronomy, 6:4–7. As parents, our primary role, above all the responsibilities that we attempt to lead out in, is carrying on the message of God to the next generation.

> Listen, Israel: The Lord our God, the Lord is one. Love the Lord your God with all your heart, with all your soul, and with all your strength. These words that I am giving you today are to be in your heart. Repeat them to your children. Talk about them when you sit in your house and when you walk along the road, when you lie down and when you get up (Deuteronomy 6:4–7).

As parents, when we read Deuteronomy 6:6, we are encouraged and compelled to get God's Word in our heart first! Everything cascades out from this truth and from our own hearts. From the internal transformation God's Word brings, we know who, and Whose, we are and then can act on the truths from God's Word. We are first and foremost followers of God. As we pass on God's truths to our children, ideally, we are doing more than just regurgitating or restating ideas we have heard from our pastor, a devotion, or a podcast. The truths from God's Word we have taken in work within our heart and soul in the nuances of who God is shaping us to be as devoted followers of Christ. This shaping is revealed in the instantaneous moments of our reaction to unexpected news, in frustrations, by joy, through discipline, the tone of our home, and in our bent toward reconciliation, forgiveness, and extending of mercy.

Because God's love moving in our hearts becomes our genuine bent and overall purpose as parents, we desire to impress the truths of God on our kids. We might see the big picture of why we are parents in a whole new way. As we clearly find our identity in Him and what He says, we become absolutely blown away by His faithfulness and love. The overriding value of our lives that will literally ooze out of who we are becomes Christ and His grand story of love, mercy, grace, purpose, and salvation!

We view the purpose of family through a new refined lens and understand our parenting can consistently echo the gospel. We allow the Lord to shape the decisions we make in the moment and the direction we are headed as a family. Our kids are watching, deciphering, and learning in our family's living laboratories how the gospel intersects life, and we as parents get to be on the front lines of our kids' discovery!

Our kids are watching, deciphering, and learning in our family's living laboratories how the gospel intersects life, and we as parents get to be on the front lines of our kids' discovery!

Carrying the message of God to our children stands out among all other responsibilities. We need to pause for just a moment on this thought. We will teach our children to walk, talk, eat, learn math, ride a bicycle, drive a car, put on their seat belt, wash dishes, a strong work ethic, patience, caring for others, etc. … the list is so long! But nothing comes even close to our calling as parents to share biblical truths with them as we do life every day. God invites us into this monumental "baton passing" of truth! What a privilege.

I know that for many of us, our kids choosing the Lord and turning toward Him can feel like an enormous burden of responsibility—know that we ultimately can't make the decision for Christ for them. But God built into the family design the plan of parents to impress the things of the Lord onto the minds and hearts of our children. This is not the sole responsibility of the church. We need to lean into that calling and His grace and mercy, as much as we can, understanding the role God has given to us in cultivating our children's hearts toward the things of God, and trusting Him with the outcome.

The Opportunity and Setting of Family

The practice of family discipleship is not simply a "box" that we jump in and out of. We don't turn it on and off. Let me put it this way; we shouldn't think we can. Family discipleship is not relegated to a Tuesday night family Bible study or a prayer time with your kids before bed. The discussions we have riding home from church can't be the only times we are discipling our kids.

- Family is an ongoing and enduring framework where discipleship occurs in real time as life happens in the extraordinary and the ordinary of family life.
- Family is a backdrop to showcase a group of individuals with different roles in lifelong relationship and who know each other

> **Family is an ongoing and enduring framework where discipleship occurs in real time as life happens in the extraordinary and the ordinary of family life.**

well authentically grappling with God's redemptive love.

The church's small group experience is different. In that case we do, in a sense, jump in and out of a Bible study on a week-to-week basis and are often guided by a set curriculum. Of course, this is important and meets needs. The family's involvement in a local church body is vital to everyone's spiritual growth for understanding the broader biblical community, engaging in corporate worship, and being on mission. But as parents, we don't wait for the church programs to script out everything our kids need spiritually. The church and the home each have a designed role. The family's design brings authenticity to the daily life of what living as a Christian might look like.

> **Family is a backdrop to showcase a group of individuals with different roles in lifelong relationship and who know each other well authentically grappling with God's redemptive love.**

This living curriculum of family life works vibrantly when we as parents make wise choices leading our children, live out the biblical calling in our lives, and we find ourselves carrying the hallmarks of Christ as we teach our children through our obedience. This obedience is not just showcased because we occasionally have planned devotions or family Bible studies, but it's on constant display in the daily choices we make that reveals God's work in our lives as parents. Know this: beauty also shines just as vibrantly in the times we fall short in our parenting, we completely mess up, and even when we fuss at our kids unfairly in our mistaken read on a situation.

The family's design brings authenticity to the daily life of what living as a Christian might look like.

In those moments of messing up we can model to our children vulnerability, restoration, asking for forgiveness, and demonstrating the need for grace and mercy. The family setting becomes the place our children can live within an authentic enactment of God's Word intersecting daily life. This is displayed in the best of times and for sure can be during those moments when we just completely blow it. Through the years, those moments of restoration after I have messed up (and for me as a driven and stubborn dad, there have been many opportunities to restore because of the mess I can create) have been some of the sweetest and life-giving moments when my daughters can see the gospel on display.

To be honest, as parents, we are discipling our kids in something every day. We can't get away from it, nor do we want to. Our lives, choices, habits, and literal words will shout a message about what we deem important. Our kids will know how we view the importance of athletics, our job, how and where

The family setting becomes the place our children can live within an authentic enactment of God's Word intersecting daily life.

we spend money, time together as family, involvement in a local church, entertainment choices, praying as a family or not, and the list goes on by the choices we make daily with words and actions. We are impressing our convictions upon them with the messages we express, and not just speak. As parents, what are those convictions your kids might be picking up from you by the way you live out your priorities?

Because of this opportunity for stewardship, let's embrace the design of family, lean into the Lord for understanding and strength in the good, the mess of our lives, the lack of knowledge in what to do, the times we are completely exhausted, and let's shout a message with our influence that is all about God. We can take courage knowing parents who know Christ in communities and cultures all around the world undertake this same biblical challenge, many at great cost. We are in this together!

The Place You Find Yourself as a Family, Start There!

While in the early days of college in east Tennessee, several of us were driving toward the Smoky Mountains trying to locate a certain area close to Gatlinburg. All new to the area, we got lost and confused. (I'm not sure Google Maps was even a dream yet.) I was tasked to ask some older gentlemen sitting in front of an old classic country general store in rocking chairs if they, by chance, knew how to get where we needed to go. Just a simple request for directions. One of the men said yes, thought for a second, tried several times to give me directions but then finally got to a point of frustration and just said... "You know, you just can't get there from here." I paused for a few seconds with a confused stare and said, "thank you." I got back in the car and we all just laughed.

In a similar way, I believe this is how we all feel sometimes as parents when challenged to parent intentionally and to biblically disciple our kids. We believe the lie that we "can't get there from where we are." So, we might have a "want to" or feel that we should, but don't go any further than that. The truth is, we begin where we are. That's the place we start from. We take one step at a time, making decisions that create movement forward. The place you find yourself as a family, start there!

The place you find yourself as a family, start there!

Leading Our Kids to a Sunrise

One summer weekend a few years back, our family hiked up Mt. LeConte in the Great Smoky Mountains National Park and stayed a night in one of the cabins on the top for registered guests. It had always been on my bucket list. We had researched what things to be sure to do when you stay there. Early the next morning, we got up well before sunrise and hiked about a mile to a lookout called Myrtle Point. We settled on a rock with a few others, faced east, and waited. What a breathtaking experience as we witnessed one of the most glorious sunrises we have seen anywhere! The sun's rays pierced the darkness and lit up the spectacular sky with majestic reds, yellows, pinks, and oranges. An epic moment for sure!

Now, let's back up about two hours and walk through the reality of events before that epic moment. The alarm went off in what we felt like was fifteen minutes after we went to bed. We all struggled to get out of our warm beds in a cold cabin, stiff and tired after yesterday's hike. The darkness felt thick and damp as we stepped off the cabin porch onto that rocky trail, and we had one flashlight to brighten up the path for all of us. It was rough, and to be honest, we each at times wanted to just turn around and go back to bed. But we had heard it was going to be amazing, so we pressed on in the night heading toward an awaiting view that seemed forever away. And, of course, we were blown away by the view and never doubted that it was worth it.

Let's compare this to our parenting. Oh, how many times we find ourselves in a cold cabin, trying to get our kids up from a slumber that takes on many facets, walking in the dark toward a view of God that's hard to recognize in the immediate chaos of our homes, and stubbing our toes on things on the dark muddled path that we find ourselves on. This is where vision and intentional parenting comes in, steers our commitment, and gives us a resolve to keep going. In our hearts and minds, we know to expect the view of God and the beauty of moments that will cause everybody to see Him as epic!

Let's do all we can to get our kids to a place to see God on display—and let Him do His work!

In those moments, you, and your whole family, will see it as worth it! Let's bring our kids to places (physical, mental, and spiritual) where they can watch and marvel at who God is—even if we have to fight the apathy, the hard choices, walking in the dark, and hard-to-see seasons. We have assured hope of the coming dawn. Let's lead our families to face toward the east, sit, and wait in expectation for the sunrise that will come! Let's do all we can to get our kids to a place to see God on display—and let Him do His work!

Relationship Is the Key Ingredient

In the coming chapters, we will begin to look at the power of our words as parents—and take a deeper dive using eight statements. We will also key in on another important effort of parents—the message in the actions of our lives found in our relationships with our kids must line up with the words we speak. They work in tandem, with one giving weight and credence to the other. I'm not talking about a surface-thick relationship of simple familiarity with each other because we live in the same house, ride in the same car, or maybe even eat together in the same room. Nor is relationship found in just making basic provisions for our kids, such as a bed, food, clothes, maybe a car, or a phone. If we aren't attentive to the depth or strength of our relationship with our kids, we can be swayed into a presumption that all is good. Are we doing all we need to do to know them and maintain a safe communication channel? How do we not slide into complacency, believing that just providing things is "good enough"?

When a strong relationship is built—or being built—between the parent and the child, this connection becomes the backdrop for the parent's influence to take root in the heart of the child.

The Backdrop for Influence

When a strong relationship is built—or being built—between the parent and the child, this connection becomes the backdrop for the parent's influence to take root in the heart of the child. The words a parent says will have a lasting impact when framed within a healthy relationship. A child must know he or she has a place where they belong, are known, and are included within a bond that is prioritized above careers, our friends, and even our pursuit of a particular lifestyle. Please hear me—this is one of the main points that I want you to understand and gain a resolve to reach. A healthy relationship with your kids is primary! The quality of the relationship you have with your child is the vehicle that delivers anything you might attempt to pass on to them.

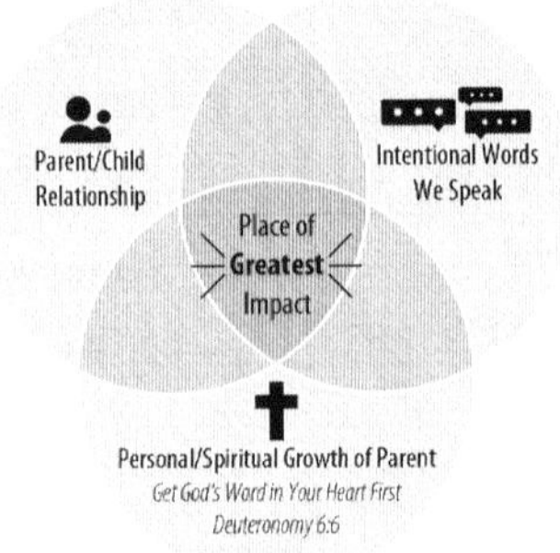

RELATIONSHIP—a rapport with someone that is based on the quality of time spent with them, hearing their hearts, asking questions, learning about their lives (and following up with further questions because we are interested), inviting them on shared experiences, creating memories of ordinary moments and grand adventures, and more.

In my 25 years of student ministry, I heard too many times from students that they hoped their parents would spend time with them instead of just providing things for them—no matter the degree to which these parents might have provided for them. So many of these students longed for a relationship with parents that led to times spent in one-on-one moments, undistracted from the tasks of life, and sitting "with" them listening and not having their parents fix anything. Students felt this was especially true related to their fathers.

RELATIONSHIP—a rapport with someone that is based on the quality of time spent with them, hearing their hearts, asking questions, learning about their lives (and following up with further questions because we are interested), inviting them on shared experiences, creating memories of ordinary moments and grand adventures, and more.

As fathers, we can often assume we are doing what we need to do because we give our kids things. But "doing what we need to do" is most strongly found in pursuing a relationship with our kids. We want a rapport with them based on time spent with them, hearing their hearts, asking questions, learning about their lives (and following up with further questions because we are interested), inviting them on shared experiences, creating memories of ordinary moments and grand adventures, and more.

Throughout my student minister years when sitting down with parents who came to me and asked for guidance with their teenager (after asking and hearing the heart of their salvation story and their child's salvation story), I first asked them to unpack the relationship they have with their child. The quality of the health of their relationship with their child creates the trajectory of how I might speak into the dynamic of the home and encourage them. If trust exists between a parent and child, the approach moving forward looks like walking side by side, looking forward together at the issue at hand even though it might be messy. If trust doesn't exist between the parent and child, it may look more like both locking horns and digging in heels in defiance. I hope you hear from me that your relationship with your child is big, and your influence and impact reverberate out from that.

Be characterized by pursuing your kids; enter their world; listen; invite them along; let them know you see them; speak words of encouragement. Push through the awkwardness, the lack of care you might receive back, the resistance, or sometimes absence of cooperation to continue building a relationship and see the bigger and longer view of things that most likely only you can see.

Four Quick Reminders for Pursuing a Relationship With Your Child

1. Have Fun Together

Look for ways to play together. Your family members gaining awareness of you desiring to be together just for the sake of being together is irreplaceable. Being told you love being with them is important, but grasping the sense of you wanting to be with them because they experience it is massive.

2. Keep Focused on the Why

Crafting moments to be together and build memories might be difficult at times, but it's worth it. As parents, we must see the bigger picture of why we do things together.

When our kids were younger, we decided to go pick blueberries. We all hopped in the car and found a great place someone had told us about. Everything was good, except it was hot, sunny, and we were accompanied by a ton of flying and crawling insects! Our kids were all letting us know that they were absolutely miserable and were not having fun. After a discouraging time of hearing them complaining while we sweat through our shirts, we left with a small bushel. My wife and I shared a look, "well, that didn't go as planned." That's what we thought anyway. Before the blueberry pie was all gone, they all said they wanted to go back and pick blueberries again, talking about how much fun they all had. What? We soon realized that being together for them was so impactful they somehow forgot how miserable they were. The Blueberry Patch Principle was born that day for us—no matter how the kids are acting in the moment, we need to remember we are guiding them on a bigger journey to create memories. We can trust the process. It's totally worth the sweat and bugs!

No matter how the kids are acting in the moment, we need to remember we are guiding them on a bigger journey to create memories.

3. Experience Versus Efficiency

Quite often, the tension is real between fashioning an experience of being together and functioning with efficiency. Remember when we play together as a family, the primary goal is to build relationships much more than simply to finish the task with proficiency. Many of us are driven in our jobs (or from within) to produce, which conditions how we might relate at home. A fishing trip can mean so much more than catching fish when a father recognizes the value of time spent with his son or daughter.

4. Turn Off the Screens

Pick a set-time period during each night, or one night a week, to turn off all screens. Prioritize eye-to-eye contact and sharing of stories. The objective is not time occupying in the same room but in conversation with each other.

Chapter 4

Five Common Obstacles in Parenting With Purpose

As we continue to explore practical steps toward building a stronger relationship with your child and offer some prompts for conversations and words to be spoken, let's take a look at common obstacles that may become evident in your home. Obstacles don't have to inhibit—they help us explore the beautiful opportunity we have and strengthen the resonating of the gospel in our daily family life. The gospel can resound out in not only the beautiful days of family, but also smack in the middle of the mess of our homes.

When I encounter traffic on the road, the extent of my frustration or determination depends on where I'm going. Yes, the time I'm supposed to arrive plays a factor in my level of resolve to find a way around obstacles, but it's really the importance I place on where I'm going that affects the level of fortitude I use to figure it out. If I'm meeting someone for lunch at noon and I hit traffic, I have a resolve to find

> **The gospel can resound out in not only the beautiful days of family, but also smack in the middle of the mess of our homes.**

another route to try to make it on time. Or, if I'm leaving the house for a staff meeting, I'm leading at the church and there is traffic, I'll do what I can to get there. If I'm just out doing errands or picking up something at the store, then it's not that important and I'll just deal with it when it comes.

When we become determined to reach a goal and then encounter obstacles along the way, the strength of our determination inspires us to clear the obstacles. Seeing the value behind an idea or a conviction causes us to press on no matter what. Belief in a truth can easily remain merely an aspiration; valuing a truth leads toward implementation.

We don't simply do what we *believe*, we do what we *value*!"
—Gregg Matte, Senior Pastor Houston's First Baptist Church

If we value addressing the needs our kids are experiencing, we will be much more willing to meet the obstacles head on and overcome them in order to really know our kids and speak into their lives with intention.

Why are we talking about obstacles in parenting before we even talk about what we can be saying to our kids? Naming the obstacles we face (or sometimes ignore) is helpful. Let's not pretend they aren't reality in our lives, but rather confront them head on. Some of these obstacles are believing you are overwhelmed with crunches in time and resources, feeling inadequate, feeling disqualified, and not knowing how to move forward because it wasn't modeled to you.

We don't simply do what we believe, we do what we value!"
—Gregg Matte, Senior Pastor Houston First Baptist

Recognizing the obstacles helps us all see and realize we are not alone. We are all together in this great story—this epic calling—of passing on the greatest story in history, past or future! Let's all be honest and own the obstacles rising in our story of parenting. When we strongly value purposeful parenting, our effort and resolve to put action steps into place to lead and impress the things of God on the hearts of our children give us a stronger resolve to work around any barriers.

Be encouraged as a parent to lead your children intentionally, no matter the backdrop lurking in the back of your mind and heart that might impede this effort. My wife and I are parents of three daughters and have been in so many difficult situations of our own. We are fully aware of how messy it all can be. We also get the moments when we feel completely inadequate. Hopefully, any overwhelming feelings you might have can be demystified, and hesitations can be diminished. Let's release assumptions that discipleship in the home is only for the spiritual elite or for the ones that entirely have it all together. It's amazing how many believe these falsehoods! As you discover some of the obstacles in your life, I pray the intensity of them begins to fall away and God does something incredible in your life.

Five Common Obstacles to Parenting With Purpose

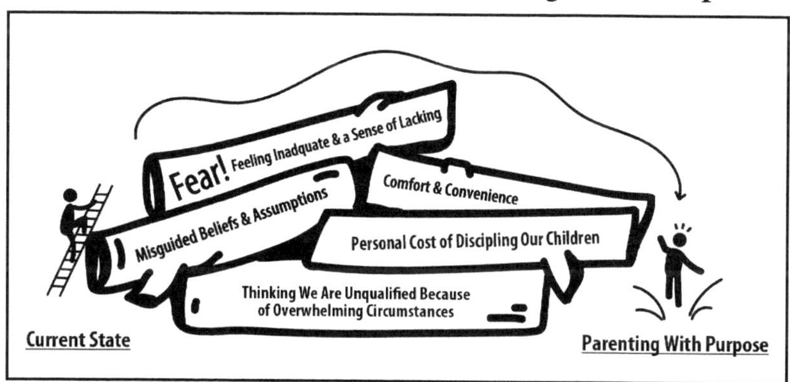

1. **The Personal Cost of Discipling Our Children**
2. **Comfort and Convenience**
3. **FEAR—Feeling Inadequate and Sense of Lacking Too Much**
4. **Thinking We Are Unqualified to Lead Our Family Because of Unique or Overwhelming Circumstances**
5. **We Are Guided by Assumptions or Misguided Beliefs About the Purpose of Family**

Obstacle 1 in Parenting With Purpose

The Personal Cost of Discipling Our Children

When I mention personal costs, I'm not actually talking about money. I'm referring primarily to the cost of a parent's time and attention. The level of pull and tug on parents from so many voices, opinions, and demands is at an all-time high. We are tempted to give our availability and attentiveness away from the important things. Time is like money, in that, we can only spend each amount once. The availability of so much information on our phones, constant interruptions of messages from culture that are promoted as imperative, or the pressing needs of the moment can all pull our attention away from leaning into our primary role as parents.

Costs that are always pulling for our time and attention.

- *I don't have time.*
- *I don't see the importance of this in light of what I view as priorities for my children—such as school, getting scholarships, college, and career.*
- *We are so wrapped up in the immediate that's all I can see.*
- *We are wrapped up in the things of culture and what it has to offer.*

- *Many parents believe, or have been unintentionally taught, that this calling of going with the gospel is the church's role, not ours as a parent and family.*
- *Distractions—(phone, friends, chores, work, etc.)*

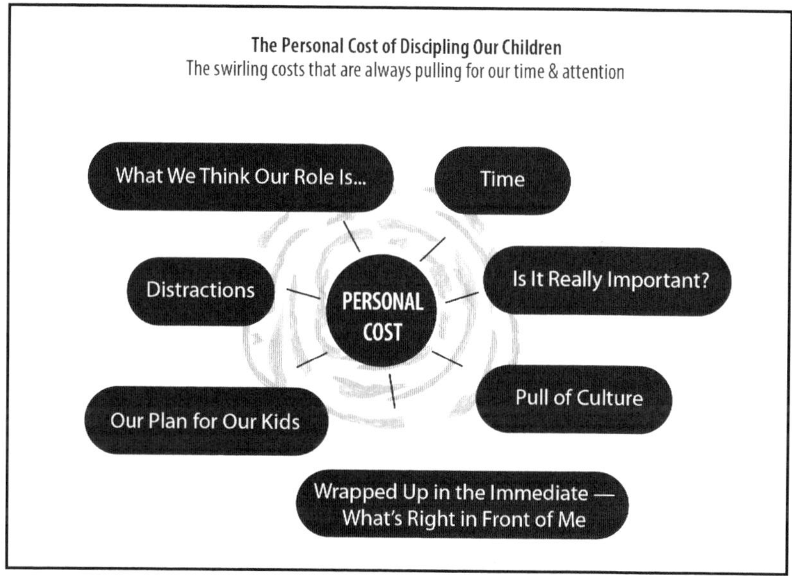

Looking at some of the personal costs to us as parents gives us perspective if we decide to be all in with leading our kids spiritually. We might need to say "no" to more things than we thought in order to find time and attention for our kids. This is a reality and often a battle. Many important things are saying "look at me, I am worthy of your attention." And they all have shiny and enticing things about them to cause us to take a glance, which is almost never just a glance. On top of that, culture says all those things are worth it. But let's be clear. To lead your entire family toward an ongoing setting to showcase God's redemptive love is costly—but worth it! A hundred years from now, and even into eternity, the spiritual grounding of our families will still be bearing fruit long after the things we often

We aren't just called to accommodate Jesus into our family's lives when we feel like it, we are to bring Him all the way in, to all areas.

attend to, instead have wasted away. We must lay down certain things to carve out our time and our attention span, especially at first when we are building a new rhythm of living life. We aren't just called to accommodate Jesus into our family's lives when we feel like it, we are to bring Him all the way in, to all areas.

We are confronted with decision points when each of us chooses to lay down the immediate and temporary tasks before us to take up the mantle of intentionally pouring into our kids. Choices are being made in the best of times and the hardest of times. When we are tired, distracted by our phones, engage in conversations with others, or have other things on our plate we are making choices. Let's be aware so we can choose well.

The Exceptional Life for Our Kids

Big decision points will come when we release plans we have for our kids, make choices to go against the pull of culture that is so prevalent, and view our parenting decisions through the lens of God's eternal plan. Can this be adventurous and exciting? Absolutely! It will be the most rewarding journey you can go on with your family. I think many adopt the belief that influencing one's family in the things of God is boring and predictable. We can be influenced to believe that if we take our eyes off what "really matters" in getting ahead (education, sports, career trajectory, lifestyle choices, etc.) to make it in this world, our kids will be left behind in those areas. Before long conversations about God, the wonder of His creation, Scripture, and prayer are squeezed out of our routine, ordinary days. We all want our kids to live an exceptional life. But what is the makeup of that exceptional life? Who will we allow to determine the answer?

Teach a Child

My maternal grandfather was wise and full of pithy statements most of our extended family remembers to this day. He would often say with a chuckle after a prayer at our meal (especially at Thanksgiving)– "if you go away hungry, it's your own fault." Another memorable statement he was known to say literally spoke into our parenting approach and how we led our girls on adventures in the outdoors. My granddad would say, "Teach a child to love nature and they'll never be bored." What a true statement! Growing up camping and playing in the forests, I know it to be true. I saw it play out in my girls as they loved hiking, learning the types of leaves, climbing trees, exploring the creeks for salamanders or crayfish, building forts with branches, throwing rocks, and creating endless games and imagined worlds outside.

Let me rephrase that statement just a bit to say, "teach a child to love being on mission and they'll never be bored." It doesn't matter which career they choose or the vocation they decide on, the world is the wide-open field for mission to unfold. This is the adventure of a lifetime! As parents, we need to make sure we let go of the plan we have already set out for them. The plan we have ordered for their life might be in contradiction to the trajectory the Lord is calling them toward. Or our tendency is to think too little on this challenge to GO and box it into our limited understanding and past experiences. And to be honest, our understanding can be underwhelming.

If we don't see the grand picture of the gospel and the design of family, we can easily be swept away by what the world states as important. That's why growing oneself in the Lord is critical. Studying and engaging in the Scriptures forms our understanding of what is crucial in life, allowing our priorities to take shape and guide us to points of decision, as we lead and influence our kids and choose how to spend the time given to us.

Five Questions That Help to Prioritize Parenting Choices

- **Who defines what really matters in your parenting choices?**
- **What are the top four outcomes in your child's life that you would view as successful parenting?**
- **How do you prioritize the decisions you make in how you lead your family?**
- **What are the top four important elements that makes up successful parenting? The challenge is to do this through the lens of the gospel and eternity.**
- **Do you actually have time to lead your children spiritually? Yes, but you have to say no to those things that are eating up your time.**

Is there a cost in leading our kids intentionally and making the choices to create a reservoir of time and resources to be with them and impress God's truth onto their hearts? Yes! But the rewards that come out of that cost can be transformational and eternal.

Obstacle 2 in Parenting With Purpose

Our Comfort and Convenience

Comfort and convenience are a personal cost that needs its own category. We want to do what we want to do. The ease of our lives is an enormous obstacle for some of us in realizing the role and opportunity we have been given. Is it easier to just drift through the foundational parenting years when our children are young and they still live in our home? Probably. But we can't be guided by ease or a path of least resistance when we are compelled to do the harder things that will shape the hearts of our children toward the heart of God. In fact, when we lean into God's plan of intentionally influencing our kids, carving out the needed time on the calendar that we think we don't have, and creating the conversations centered on the collision of faith and culture, we meet some of the greatest resistance. But it's in those moments on the harder path where the most adventurous and effective passing on of faith can happen. Relationships can deepen in the midst of those times that our kids need the most encouragement or strength to stand. Memories are built when we find ourselves present with them when they experience the joy of aha moments or the tough times when friends are boxing them out. Influence could be the strongest when they notice your availability as they walk through a tough decision, or you simply sit with them when they hurt.

Drive Across the Country

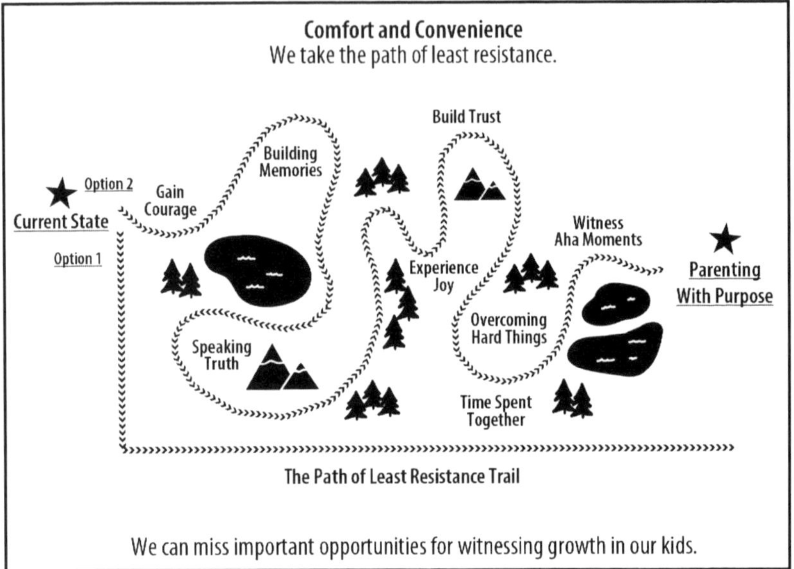

When our kids were younger, we drove across the country several times to see the great outdoors of the West. Some of this desire to go on long trips was impressed on me as my parents drove us across dozens of states throughout my childhood. My wife and I also wanted to camp along the way in tents—mostly driven by our budget constraints. Whatever the reasons, those days of watching the landscape of America roll by with my family were shared experiences that I had no idea would be so formational for us. In fact, when my kids were in their teenage years and we told them we were finally going to fly out west and not have to drive, they each initially paused and grieved a little. We were surprised, but we shouldn't have been. The memories of driving and the strength of that shared experience remain powerful.

If the choice was a cheap trip or no trip, we chose a cheap trip every time. But it also came down to a deliberate choice we made when we left our home with the destination in mind. We drove out of our driveway in Tennessee, down our street, headed toward the interstate, and simply didn't get off the interstate until we were in Utah, Wyoming, or Montana. Yes, we stopped to get food, gas, and camp along the way. But we always got back on the interstate and kept driving west. We knew the place we wanted to end up in our journey and we kept that in our view.

When we make the decision to deliberately lead our kids spiritually, we view the destination in mind. Off-ramps are always options before us. Each day we pass by countless opportunities to stop, veer off, or wander from the road of intentionality, especially if the billboards of comfort and convenience are all saying in big bright letters, EXIT NOW. But let's not be distracted! See the long view and where you want to go! Choose wisely. Let's pick our family and kids. Our time is precious—and limited—so let's choose our family and kids.

Our kids will also prayerfully begin to recognize that we are creating the margin to talk with them. We will have the temptation to let them know that we are taking time out of our busy day to spend with them, but there's no reason to tell them you are saying no to other choices to spend time with them. They know or will soon realize. And this coming awareness they will catch one day is that their parents chose them.

Obstacle 3 in Parenting With Purpose

FEAR: Feelings of Inadequacy and a Sense of Lacking Too Much

In a time when we have instant access to so many informational portals—YouTube, Podcasts, etc.—one would think we should never be without "how-to" guides and approaches to learn and do just about anything. We can put into search engines any phrase related to an issue, problem, subject, or question and we will get so many options. But the problem is not necessarily the lack of "know-how," it might be the lack of personal experience to do what is asked of us or a variety of other reasons related to this obstacle. And the fears that pop up are enormous. I can watch a how-to video of someone playing guitar and learn some basic strumming and chords and feel pretty good about it. But thinking about being up front to lead worship with a guitar in the next couple of weeks—no way!

Let's list some of the most common things we allow to create fear in our lives that keep us from moving forward with being full-on intentional in discipling our kids and engaging with kids with powerful statements that speak into their heart.

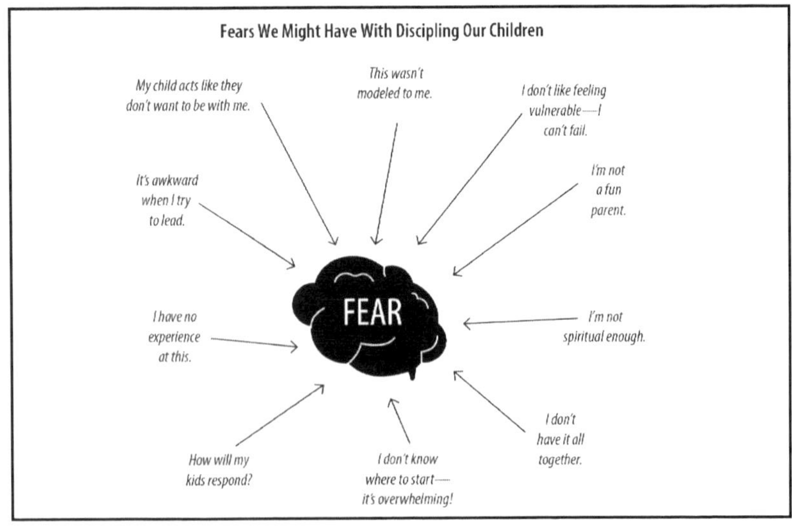

What are the things that speak into creating Fear?

- *Don't feel "spiritual" enough. We compare.*
- *Have no personal experience.*
- *What will my child's response be?*
- *Vulnerability. I don't have it all together. I can't fail.*
- *I feel inadequate to parent and lead out.*
- *I'm not a fun parent.*
- *I need very practical ways in how to implement all this—I don't know where to start. I'll need a script to follow.*
- *This is for those more spiritual families, not mine—the ones who have it all together.*
- *It's awkward when I attempt to lead out or be intentional.*
- *My child acts like they don't want to be with me.*
- *What if my child doesn't reciprocate what I'm sharing with them?*
- *This was not modeled to me from my parents, I don't know how.*
- *Parents are still working on where they find their identity; parents feel they can't say these words because they are still working on it.*

I wonder if some of the things mentioned above have been the very obstacles causing you some fear about moving forward with leading your child intentionally. Or maybe some of the ones mentioned are some sort of variation. Maybe it was a recent realization, or it was a long time ago and you haven't thought about it in a while. Maybe you read some of the things above that lead us to fear and for the first time you realize that one or two of these have become personal for you. What do we do about it? Here is my challenge:

- Name it
- Come to an agreement with the Lord that this is you
- Give it the Lord, and pray to move forward
- Have a resolve to start

In whatever manner we got to this place of fear, it can keep us from doing great things! Let's take the next step.

Walking Down a Path

My wife and I, our daughters, and now along with their husbands, love to hike. You'll hear more later about where this all came from in my life, but being out in nature, among the trees, climbing a mountain, I really get to know and observe what Paul talked about in Romans 1:20 when he wrote, "His invisible attributes, that is, his eternal power and divine nature, have been clearly seen since creation of the world, being understood through what he has made."

Trails and paths are important as they lead us on a route to experience the Lord's creative beauty and awe. And our family has collectively hiked thousands of miles through the years to some incredible places and views. But one thing I have come to understand about trails—they are all different. I mean the actual trail or path that you step on. They are either maintained or not. Sometimes they are gravel, dirt, filled with roots, or even paved at times. Sometimes they're washed out or muddy and you must navigate carefully. And some trails are grown over with grass and weeds; these are the ones you must really pay attention to because you can't see what you're stepping on.

Roots, rocks, stumps, and even the occasional bug, snake, or turtle might be underneath the grass. Anyone can surely trip, turn ankles, and look completely awkward when hiking on a path like that. But the more that type of grown-over path is hiked on by shoes and boots and stepped on hundreds of times, the more well-worn the path can become. The rocks and roots are revealed over time, and you learn how to traverse them. You might trip occasionally, but after some time it becomes more natural, and you gain confidence through the experience of walking down that path so many times because it's what you do. When someone grew up in a home that didn't model much discipleship or intentional gospel conversation, beginning to talk about God and Scripture can feel like a rocky, uneven, and obscure path. I believe this is the gradual and realistic approach parents can take when parenting with purpose, building strong relationships, and using powerful words of encouragement.

Those are "paths and trails" that maybe you haven't walked down much as you currently parent your kids. We can feel inadequate, we haven't gained much experience in being intentional, it can be awkward along the way, and you might even "trip" some. Look past the fears that might stop you and take the first few steps to move a little bit further down the trail than you were before. But the more you engage in conversations and the more often you say powerful words to your kids, the more natural and well-worn it all becomes. And for sure, the more well-worn the influence and impression of the things of God becomes as

But the more you engage in conversations and the more often you say powerful words to your kids, the more natural and well-worn it all becomes.

you parent with purpose, the more truth will be impressed upon the hearts of your kids. We need to know the reality that without a doubt no parent, no kid, and no family is perfect. But we aren't alone in the journey! Many of those same families that are approaching every fear mentioned earlier are making the choice to go for it, working through all the awkward and inadequate moments because they believe there must be more, or they see the bigger picture of God's design of family. And you can do it, too.

My Dad's Upbringing—and the Choices He Made

This is a little of my dad's story. I was fortunate enough to be led by him in our family as he and my mom built a close, relational, and cohesive family that was infused with a love for God. It wasn't picture perfect all the time or seamless in all that we did. My brothers, sisters and I sure had our fair share of arguments, and we all made a mess of things along the way, but my parents cultivated a love for the Lord in our family's relationships. But the part I really want you to understand is that my dad was not modeled on building healthy relationships or having a home that understood the power of words spoken when he was growing up in a small Texas town. He grew up in a home that looked very little like the home I grew up in.

His dad (PaPa to us grandkids) worked in hard conditions for the Santa Fe Railroad on the hot plains of Texas. PaPa had no college degree. He was raised by an uncle and aunt after his parents died when he was very young. He did his best in figuring things out by providing the basics for my dad and building a family and home in the way he knew. My dad would tell us he had strong memories of his dad being home most of the time and sitting in his chair in the living room. But PaPa's presence in the room didn't automatically turn into a healthy relationship with dad. PaPa rarely, if ever, said words to my dad that spoke into his heart and identity. In fact, he only remembers hearing the words, "I love you" from his father just a couple of times growing up.

His dad's physical proximity didn't translate into intentional words that clearly made known his affection and approval to my dad. Love for my dad might have been felt by my PaPa, but it was not clearly communicated and directed to my dad. My PaPa's story growing up and losing his parents at a young age was tragic, and one that he had no control over. Because of this, and many other factors, his lack of understanding for building family relationships was most likely passed down from his uncle and aunt and then continued to the next generation, modeled to my dad.

My dad's mom (SweetMama to us) had her own method in parenting. She was a wonderful lady to us grandkids—fun, energetic, and filled with laughter. She was kind and loved us grandkids a lot. But her approach to parenting my dad was characterized by using guilt frequently to get my dad to do things around the house. It might have been indirect or even incidental at first, but it soon became a primary method of hers that developed deep roots in my dad's heart. I took notice of this when I was in high school. It caught me off guard a little, not because she was outwardly unkind and harsh, but because it was so subtle yet obviously a pattern of manipulation that had been built over the years in her relationship with my dad.

This growing awareness of my dad's upbringing and the home that was modeled to him began to really collide with the family dynamics I was brought up in. These two homes didn't match up. My dad was incredibly intentional, built strong relationships with each of us, used words to encourage us and convey his love, and built a strong family identity with Christ at the forefront. This was obviously different from what he knew and experienced. How did he know what to do? How did he know there might be something different? Who modeled a healthy home for him? What led to his resolve to go for it, even when faced with a lack of understanding or a clear picture of what could be? I'm sure all kinds of fear were present!

He moved to flip the narrative of his family story and how healthy relationships were going to be a value. He took steps to build and foster relationships with my mom and then with us, his children. He determined it would not just be a belief or aspiration he held. Without getting into all the runway details, here are the five big steps on his journey:

Five Steps He Chose to Take

1. He *recognized* there had to be more to family relationships than what he grew up in.
2. He began to look, *observe*, listen, and would literally interview others when he noticed something different with their family. My mom's upbringing in a healthy home was huge in helping encourage him, and a letter from my maternal grandfather was pivotal in giving him assurance that he could, and was, doing it.
3. He *implemented* what he was learning. Yep, he started walking down an unfamiliar path.
4. He had a *resolve* to move forward. He had the long view in mind.
5. He *pressed* on even when it was awkward...and when he "tripped" up along the way.

He turned on a dime (or literally in one generation) from what he experienced and knew about family and pivoted toward a new and fresh way he chose to parent and build a home. He did not just casually wait and hope for a strong relational family to just happen or a family that impressed the truths of God upon each of us to simply appear.

He decided to be purposeful and *intentional* in leading his family differently from the way he was brought up. Could he have convinced himself that he had an excuse to just keep doing family like his parents? Maybe. But he didn't. He saw what family could be and he put everything toward that end. Here's what I fully believe—You can do it, too! Don't listen to the lies that you can't do it because you didn't grow up with that approach or you can't because it wasn't modeled to you.

Don't listen to the lies that you can't do it because you didn't grow up with that approach or you can't because it wasn't modeled to you.

Obstacle 4 in Parenting With Purpose

Thinking We Are Unqualified to Lead Our Family Because of Unique or Overwhelming Circumstances

Once again, if we are honest, we can find areas in our lives we might describe as a mess, chaotic, or even identify ways we have fallen short. These so-called messes or shortcomings could be created by decisions we have made, or because they were created for us by decisions of others. In fact, we can think we're the only ones who have questions and doubts.

Questions & Doubts

All parents have questions and doubts about their parenting abilities.

- *You don't understand our family—there's too much junk to work through.*
- *It's difficult—my family will not cooperate. You should see how my kids resist.*
- *My spouse is not on the same page—he/she will not participate.*
- *It's too late to start, my child is too old.*
- *Emotionally, we've not had the tools to deal with our own stuff.*

The Pile Before Me

When it comes to having projects done at our home, minor or major, I have a hard time putting into the budget the cost of labor and paying someone to do a job I know I can do. I don't mind paying for parts, supplies, or resources to complete a project at hand. But, to pay labor to someone when I think I can do just as good of a job—I'll just do it myself. My wife, over the years, has consistently said to me about whatever project is before us, "just pay someone to do it." I may have thought to do that a couple of times, but unless it's electrical or dealing with our HVAC system, I just can't let that money go from our budget. This is especially true when it comes to landscaping of any kind.

Years ago, my wife and I designed and planned to build a large patio in our backyard. We proposed to have a large area of pavers, beautiful landscaping with flowers, bushes, and even trees surrounding it, a fireplace ring in the middle, and landscape lighting all around. I was determined to do it myself. But because our yard slanted some away from our house, we first needed to build up the area with dirt and create large berms around the soon to be patio. I called a local landscape company nearby, discussed the project and the dimensions of the patio and the dynamics of our backyard, and agreed upon the amount of dirt that should be brought in as a base. With my shovel in hand, I waited patiently for the truck to appear with the dirt.

I heard the rumble of the dump truck approaching and eagerly looked up the driveway for a first glimpse. I was taken back a little at the size of it and felt my eyes glaze over at the whole scenario as it backed down my driveway. The truck positioned itself where I told the driver to dump it, and then the truck began to unload a massive mound of dirt in the middle of my yard. After unloading this pile of dirt, the truck finished its work, and I watched the truck drive up my driveway and disappear. I slowly turned around and faced this behemoth of a mound, holding my ordinary shovel in my hand, and about wept. Not sure what I was thinking when I had it delivered.

Apparently, I wasn't. What have I done? I can never do this with this shovel. I sat down in the yard, silent for a while, and then started searching on my phone for the cost of a skid steer for rent.

Nope, no way I'm paying that much for something I already set out to do by myself with no labor costs. I decided to slowly start moving the dirt around with my shovel. A little at a time. And you know what? After a couple of hours of work, I began to see enough change and shaping of the dirt, that I got more and more excited and began to believe that I could do this. I even got out my massive LED light trees to light up my entire backyard to work late into the night. (I never asked the neighbors their thoughts about this plan.) It was slow, and it took me a while to finally move all the dirt, but I did it. Step by step, shovel by shovel, I gave shape to something that I thought was too big for me to ever think I could accomplish.

Let's go back to the list of overwhelming circumstances that seem too big for us to move forward as a family. Step by step. Decision by decision. Turn over to God what needs to be turned over to Him. Look past the massive pile of circumstances that might have been dumped right in front of you and ask the Lord for the help you need. If you need to sit down, weep, and spend a period of silence with Him, take that time. You're not holding and empowering an ordinary shovel in your hand like I did when moving dirt. The Lord is the one holding you—and if we allow—it's His strength that is empowering us! No circumstances exclude you from moving forward. That's the essence of grace.

It's in these moments of feeling overwhelmed I hear the Words of Scripture shout out with truth into the situation I find myself in allowing me to move forward!

His grace is available!

God is able to make every grace overflow to you, so that in every way, always having everything you need, you may excel in every good work (2 Corinthians 9:8).

His strength is available!

Those who trust in the LORD will renew their strength; they will soar on wings like eagles; they will run and not become weary, they will walk and not faint" (Isaiah 40:31).

His forgiveness is available!

If we confess our sins, he is faithful and righteous to forgive us our sins and to cleanse us from all unrighteousness (1 John 1:9).

Reconciliation is available through Christ!

But now he has reconciled you by his physical body through his death, to present you holy, faultless, and blameless before him (Colossians 1:22).

His guidance is available!

Teach me to do your will, for you are my God. May your gracious Spirit lead me on level ground (Psalm 143:10).

The Lord is bigger than any issue you think you have!

Don't worry about anything, but in everything, through prayer and petition with thanksgiving, present your requests to God. And the peace of God, which surpasses all understanding, will guard your hearts and minds in Christ Jesus (Philippians 4:6–7).

Let Him lift you up!

The LORD is near the brokenhearted; he saves those crushed in spirit (Psalm 34:18).

You can do it—with the Lord's strength in you!

Obstacle 5 in Parenting With Purpose

We Are Driven by Assumptions and Misguided Beliefs About the Purpose of Parenting

We might not be at the place we need to be spiritually. Honestly much of our heart and obedience flows from how close we are to the Lord and the level of our submission to Him. Personal discipleship might be the primary issue that needs to be awakened. Additionally, I believe strongly we have allowed culture to define markers indicating accomplishments rather than Scripture, which impacts how we view our role as parents. Are we relying on our own opinion when it comes to "doing" family? Do we even consider where we're headed as family? When it's all said and done, is the content of our words we say to our kids preparing them for what's coming in life? Not only the right trajectory, but readying their minds and hearts for when things seem to be coming apart.

I think one of the biggest obstacles to having a great family could be that we have settled for things being good enough. Or, since we have no frame of reference or anything to compare our family dynamics to, we make the assumptions ourselves and we specify the terms of the outcome or end game. We have no idea if the walls are crooked or not because we don't have a level, an awareness that there is one, or even care to utilize it if we knew. We can drift to a place of resignation where survival is enough. We even might believe in and settle for the tie downs that someone gave us to hold down the trash in the back of the pick-up truck and we say, "that's not going anywhere," knowing that when you get above 30 mph, it's going all over the place. As long as we can prevent a complete fly apart, we must be doing fine. But are we?

We receive input from "sources" or lies, therefore our output of how we "do" parenting is affected.

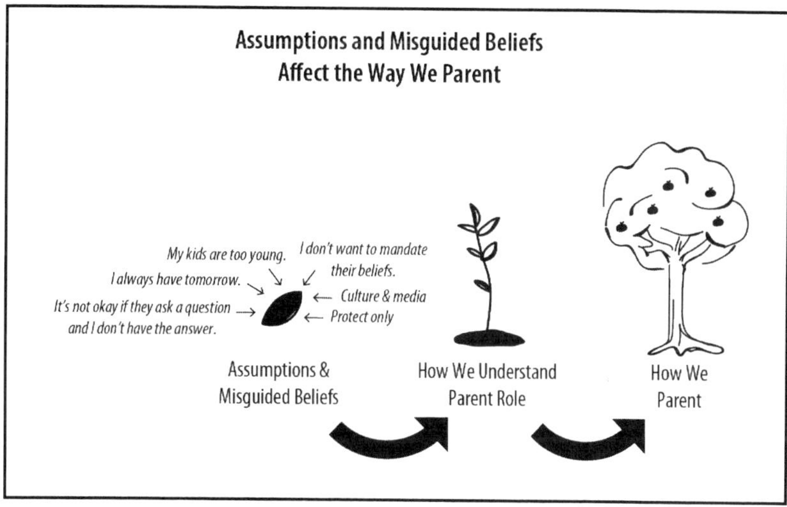

Some misguided beliefs to be aware of:

- *My kids can't understand spiritual things right now, we'll do it later.*
- *We listen to the lie that our words spoken will outweigh any actions and choices we make.*
- *The indicators we have created for successful parenting is based on what culture is telling us, and we aren't driven primarily by God's design of family.*
- *There is always more time to do this, I'll start tomorrow.*
- *I don't want to mandate and indoctrinate my kids; they need to figure it out on their own.*
- *We try to neutralize all threats. Healthy preparation of our kids' hearts and minds versus the intent to simply protect them from all threats.*

- *We stop advancing our efforts to simply go along with what others are or aren't doing.*

Read Before Opening

Many of us have been there. A new device or gadget was ordered and has finally arrived. We hurriedly open the package, glance at the clearly marked packet of directions and the bright red READ BEFORE OPENING label for just a second, and then dive in to putting together the thing you can't wait to assemble without reading the directions. But waiting is exactly what we end up doing, because in our impatience and eagerness to get the gadget going, we have overlooked the needed component or order of steps to ensure everything fits correctly into place. In our misguided attempts, we see what the completed item is supposed to look like from a picture, but we don't know the steps to put the available pieces together to make it look like that.

We may know what outcome we want when discipling kids. We can become misguided when we don't fully understand the whole picture, when we allow improper voices to speak into our understanding, or simply assume things from our limited view. Vision is important, but we are wise to guard ourselves from scripting or jumping ahead to the outcomes of parenting (which belong to God) and apply ourselves to walking with Him faithfully in the process, paying attention to the truths God has given us.

Who Decides What "Successful Parenting" Looks Like?

How are we supposed to gain an understanding of successful parenting when we are looking at the indicators created by a world that doesn't recognize that a holy God designed the family? And if those indicators aren't built around God's design, where will it lead us as we make the decisions we do as parents? We probably even lean in and turn our ears to listen to what "everybody else is doing" because that must be right, isn't it?

The Stance and Bold Proclamation of Joshua

I am captivated by the faith story and bold stance of Joshua found in Joshua 24:15. Here he stood addressing all the tribes of Israel. He was older in age, and he reminded this nation of who they are and whose they are, and challenged them to come back to the one true God. "But if it doesn't please you to worship the LORD, choose for yourselves today: Which will you worship—the gods your ancestors worshiped beyond the Euphrates River or the gods of the Amorites in whose land you are living? As for me and my family, we will worship the LORD" (Joshua 24:15).

Joshua recognized they were worshiping other gods, and he pleaded with them to return and worship the Lord. He asked, "what will you do, who will you worship?" Then he proclaimed this echoing "stake in the ground" conviction of his heart, his secure determination, "as for me and my family, we will worship the LORD." What a moment!

Joshua's own people had chosen to abandon the Lord. He defied the prevailing culture of the moment and drove a stake in the spiritual ground of his family that reverberates today. He yielded to the Spirit of God rather than being persuaded by the crowd. He saw beyond the messaging of the masses and held to the calling and obedience of the One.

Every parent will have this moment as they lead their family, an opportunity for an initial "stake in the ground" commitment of following Him above the influence and voices of the crowd around us. Our initial commitment to His design of family reverberates out and affects our daily decisions of how we do family. All our major choices and overall direction of family cascade out from this conviction of God's place in our hearts.

Our initial commitment to His design of family reverberates out and affects our daily decisions of how we do family.

Chapter 5

The Wants and Needs of Our Kids

Although growing up in my parent's home might have been more than a few years ago, I distinctly remember the things that I wanted as a child and teenager. As a child it came in the form of a Krispy Kreme doughnut on the way home from church on Sunday nights, the new blue bicycle that was at the local Toy Mart, the new Mattel video game my friend had, or learning to ski behind my granddad's boat. When I became a teenager, I wanted my driver's license so I could drive our family's green Camaro that had been passed down from my siblings who drove it before me. And I wanted gas money to go with it. I also remember striving to meet the deeper needs I had; I just wasn't quite aware of how to name them, but they were as real to me as my wants.

It's not like I could identify these needs by name when I was nine years old or make a list of how I could have them met. I couldn't write them on a board in my room and then list the ways that my parents were meeting those specific needs and grade their attempts and performances. I just sensed the longings in my heart. And I knew when needs were being met through a strong sense of belonging and being welcomed in, knowing I was valued by my parents. I knew I was loved by them, and our family loved the Lord and His church.

My parents even led us on shared adventures, building up a treasure trove of memories that became markers of our family identity. Of course, putting these feelings I had when I was a child into words and being able to write these out came a lot later in my life. But these things were happening in real time back then, whether I could name them or not. As I look back on growing up as a child in our home on that familiar street, in all the ups and downs family brought to me, the meeting of deeper needs shaped who I was then and who I am today.

If we as parents can focus first on meeting the needs of our kids, we can speak to the deeper parts of our child, which builds trust, hope, and healthy confidence.

WANTS: Desires that are closer to the surface of an individual's mind if asked: entertainment, technology, food, freedom, or whatever their friends have.

NEEDS: Below the surface longings that are deeper in the hearts and souls of an individual.

Wants are mostly visible above the water. Needs are below the water and often out of sight.

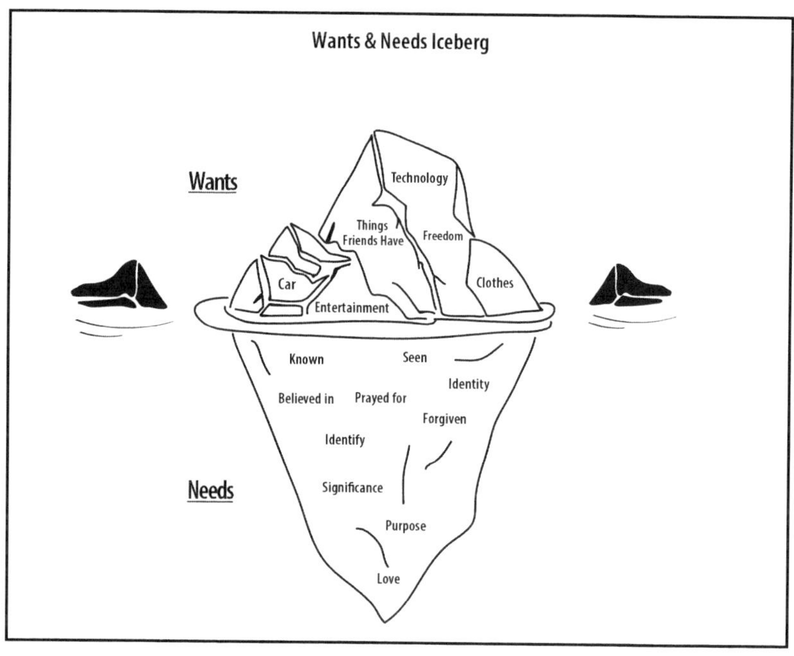

Kids can name most of what they want. On the other hand, most, if not all, of what our kids need is hidden from our view in their hearts and minds. But we must know the needs are real, and the search is on by our kids to have them met. Some wants are also needs, but we can recognize important differences between the two when talking about Wants of kids and the depth of the crucial Needs of their hearts they strive to satisfy.

If we as parents can focus first on meeting the needs of our kids, we can speak to the deeper parts of our child, which builds trust, hope, and healthy confidence. Prayerfully they begin to gain a healthy understanding of identity, purpose, and reconciliation.

Ultimately, complete identity, purpose, and reconciliation are found and grounded through faith in Christ and the finished work on the Cross—all needs are fully met in Him. But the family can begin to echo the truths of the gospel as we practice our faith at home, impressing biblical truth upon the lives of our kids. Meeting our kids' deeper needs feeds their hungriest God-given appetites.

The Wants are those desires that are closer to the surface of a kids' mind. If asked they might list entertainment, electronics, food, freedom, or whatever their friends have. In fact, without being asked, kids clamor for what they want. We can see past the clamor to the needs underneath. The Needs I hope to identify in the coming chapters are those longings residing deeper in the hearts and souls of a kid. They might not be able to name it as clearly as they would a certain device they crave, but the search for fulfilling these Needs is more real and desperate. Kids seek fulfillment of needs such as belonging, being seen, believed in, being loved, and being longed for. If not intentional and deliberate, parents can find themselves only working to meet the immediate and visible Wants of their kids, and not understanding the opportunity we have to recognize and address the deeper and below-the-surface Needs that can drastically change so much in the hearts of our kids and our family.

Guiding Our Kids to Christ

When discerning our kids' needs seems difficult or new, it helps to remember only Jesus can meet all their needs. But we are uniquely placed by God as their parents to see what no one else can see and perceive our kids more thoroughly than any friend ever could. Nothing on this side of Heaven is perfect and flawless. We will still miss needs and be wrong sometimes. We won't parent with intention every minute. But we can know in the trenches of real life, that grace and redemption through God's design of family is on display and He is at work in both the days of parenting when every decision seems to land on point and in the moments of utter indecisiveness and feeling insufficient. Ultimately parents can lead their kids toward the fullness of these needs being fulfilled in Jesus. I'm thankful to the core He doesn't require perfection from us to do this. He asks for our faithfulness and attentiveness to the task, promising to equip and sustain us all the way.

As we parent, let's lean into this idea of Wants and Needs, recognizing the differences and necessity of both. Allow this understanding to fuel your efforts within your family and help you settle on specifics for how you might address some deeper needs of each child. Think in terms of your own deeper needs, and how they are met in Christ. Through our relationships and words that we speak we lead ourselves and our children to Jesus, who will ultimately satisfy all of our deepest needs.

The family has an opportunity to give a foretaste of the gospel story and many of its attributes.

Family: Echoing the Message of the Gospel

Within the overall design of family, opportunities will occur in the ebb and flow of relationships and ordinary days for truths of the gospel to whisper into the hearts of our children. Meeting needs in the family draws a tangible picture of biblical values, now experienced partially, one day to be completed in Christ. The family has an opportunity to give a foretaste of the gospel story and many of its attributes.

Gospel impact can be on full display to feel, explore, and understand through experience, not just read as words on a page. As we live out family intentionally with Christ's life as the basis for all we do, the values of forgiveness, belonging, identity, love, and God as defender are woven throughout each unique family's daily life and experienced by every family member.

Gospel truths family can echo:

Belonging to Him!

> Acknowledge that the Lord is God. He made us, and we are his—his people, the sheep of his pasture (Psalm 100:3).

Being welcomed to a place in a family allows individuals to sense belonging, like having a place at the dinner table. As believers in Christ, we belong to God and His family. The beautiful picture and illustration that the Lord used throughout Scripture is through the relationship of sheep and their shepherd. Being in His pasture, we are cared for by Him. We belong to Him, and we have a place that we are known and seen.

We all have a role!

> Now you are the body of Christ, and individual members of it (1 Corinthians 12:27).

We each have a role in a family, and this is also true within the body of Christ where everyone will have gifts that work in unity. We have a place we can contribute toward a greater purpose.

These are my people!

> So, then, you are no longer foreigners and strangers, but fellow citizens with the saints, and members of God's household (Ephesians 2:19).

Identity can be shaped by those we share life with. As members of households, both human and as a part of God's family, we have been received into a community that shares distinctive characteristics. "These are my people" proclaims shared values, beliefs, and a common core.

The call of family!

> For God loved the world in this way: He gave his one and only Son, so that everyone who believes in him will not perish but have eternal life (John 3:16).

> But you will receive power when the Holy Spirit has come on you, and you will be my witnesses in Jerusalem, in all Judea and Samaria, and to the ends of the earth (Acts 1:8).

The beauty of the gospel message is the invitation that is given to all to come. As a family, we can unite around this message of repentance and salvation that is found in Christ. These verses can serve as a family mission statement, stating an eternal purpose to guide all decisions of that family. This is who we are! Parents understand the key role they have in carrying on the message of the gospel to the next generation.

What is love?

> Love is patient, love is kind. Love does not envy, is not boastful, is not arrogant, is not rude, is not self-seeking, is not irritable, and does not keep a record of wrongs. Love finds no joy in unrighteousness but rejoices in the truth. It bears all things, believes all things, hopes all things, endures all things. Love never ends. But as for prophecies, they will come to an end; as for tongues, they will cease; as for knowledge, it will come to an end (1 Corinthians 13:4–8).

The family can live out the true definition of love that is found in 1 Corinthians. In a world that has redefined love as lust, how a family relates can show biblical love lived out. Although perfect love is only lived out through Christ, family can be a unit characterized by showing love consistently.

Let's pray!

> Devote yourselves to prayer; stay alert in it with thanksgiving (Colossians 4:2).

Jesus would often temporarily pull away from His followers and the massive crowds to be alone with the Father in prayer. Parents can model authentic prayer. Prayers within the family can be deeply intimate especially considering the close proximity of family, shared burdens, and trust found in strong relationships.

Chapter 6

Framing-Up the Eight Statements

Now that we have taken an honest look at where we are at home, reaffirmed the importance of the quality of our relationships with our kids, considered their deeper needs and realized obstacles, let's unpack and explore eight impactful statements that we as parents must express to our children to begin to meet the deeper needs they have. Yes, they are easy statements, but the message that resonates out is bigger than we can imagine. We can examine two things: Are these messages we believe are important? If we do, would our kids say they consistently receive these messages from us?

Our relationships provide the backdrop for our kids to lean into the words we speak even more.

Remember, the magnitude of the influence our homes carry in meeting the needs our children strive to satisfy cannot be overstated. Addressing deeper needs works in tandem with the words we are speaking, which helps to build a healthy relationship. Our relationships provide the backdrop for our kids to lean into the words we speak even more.

We will also explore the counterfeit messages and lies from culture that our children could be vulnerable to, and the danger of assumptions we might make as we relate to our kids. Our attention to the wide expanse of discipleship in the home might need to be refreshed. Therefore, the goal and purpose are to lead you on a journey toward a renewed view and strong understanding of family discipleship that inspires you and shapes a determination for practical action steps.

Don't Unload All the Statements at Once and Expect Impact

Hopefully it's evident these statements won't be effective said once and then checked off as done. We can't decide for all the kids to come down to the family room on some random Monday night, asking them to sit on the sofa, and then read the statements to them from a piece of paper. Nor do we need to ask if anyone has any questions about the statements you just read to them. These statements have exponentially more weight when done organically and in ordinary situations of family life, spontaneously, and in the daily trenches. Have patience with yourself and your kids moving forward if this approach of speaking encouraging words is completely new in your home.

When I cook on the stove, my wife often reminds me to not turn it on HIGH every time. I want to knock it out and get the food cooked. But I know that if I'm on the grill, or my sons-in-law are smoking meat on their smokers a slow heat is required for the best brisket or chicken.

Start and press on, knowing the changes will be worth it. Your family story is continuing to be written and refreshed!

Framing Up

Here are some steps that can help you frame up the condition of your heart as you read.

Pause and Pray

—that God will teach and inspire your understanding. Be real with Him.

Read and Listen

—to the heartbeat of your family and to what God is teaching you through His Word and Spirit.

Learn

—and lean into and seek understanding. The simplest things can be most easily overlooked or disregarded.

Adjust

—learn how to alter your parenting approach where needed.

Be Honest

—by not holding back anything in what you tell God. Go big and be authentic in what you ask!

Take Risks

—and fight through the awkwardness, the feelings of inadequacies, and the newness of it all.

Laugh

—when it doesn't go well—yes, laugh! And keep going.

Be Vulnerable

—and real with your kids.

Share

—with your spouse or others what is resonating in your heart.

Pause

—and be observant of openings to speak words of encouragement into the hearts of your children.

Allow

—space for God to work. Feel free to stop and think, journal, pray, or just sit with what God is teaching you.

Chapter 7

Statement #1 "I'm So Glad You're in Our Family!"

Other ways to say it: *"I love doing life with you!"/ "Yay, you're here!"/ "I am so happy we are a family."/ "How cool that God chose us to be family together."*

The Need Being Met: A place to belong, be known, and have healthy relationships. We are created with a need to belong, which illustrates our need to belong to God.

Having a Role / Knowing I Had a Place

As I alluded to earlier, growing up with my mom, dad, and siblings, we camped and hiked a lot. I'm not just talking about hiking in local city parks or camping in the closest state parks, although we did that. Our type of camping, and often backpacking, usually involved driving across the country from our home in Tennessee and exploring National Parks, National Forests, and many western landscapes. My dad went big! It's what he did, so therefore we all did. In my earliest memories of backpacking as a family, I believe I was around five years old. We hiked every summer in the Sangre

De Cristo mountains of New Mexico north of Sante Fe in the Holy Ghost Canyon area.

We would set out on the trail for a five-day adventure to backpack a seven to eight-mile journey, stopping halfway for a night to set up our tents, and then continuing up (up, up, and more up) to Lake Stewart. We each had a role and responsibility of things to carry. I remember the feeling that I was a part of a grand adventure and that this group on the trail with me were my people. Hiking together on the mountain trail within the six members of our family, I sensed a strong place of belonging. Doing hard things in the middle of a forest, carrying a backpack, going uphill (both ways, of course) and playing my part in bringing either food or tent poles, I had a place.

Belonging is one of the deepest needs each person has. The search for a group to join, be invited into, and enthusiastically welcomed is major. To know we can and will fit in, in any type of setting, at just about any age, is a constant search that propels us all. Each of us can most likely remember looking for belonging back in the elementary years when we got our food in the cafeteria, held our tray, and slowly searched around intently looking for our group of friends that hopefully saved a seat for us. In middle and high school years, finding friends that will accept us and bring us along drives us every day. As adults during the work lunch breaks, we wonder who might invite us today or this week to join them.

This desire to identify with a group was even evident when I had a Jeep CJ5 back in college. I was a part of a community of other Jeep owners that I didn't even know about until I had one, and I didn't really know I desired it until it started happening. I discovered the two-finger wave from the steering wheel all Jeep owners somehow know when passing each other on two lanes roads. The search to be included is all over and in the least expected places.

The family plays a massive role in helping meet this need. Belonging in family can meet a lifelong need, and significantly lower the inner sense of desperation to find others with which to belong.

Words Spoken in the Margins

Although moments like hiking with my family were powerful because of the experience itself, the words spoken by my parents while we were backpacking gave weight to what I was experiencing. Both my parents spoke intentional words and statements to us as children that met a deeper need for belonging. On those hiking trips while sitting around the campfire, they would take opportunities to say phrases like "I'm so happy we're in the same family" and "I love doing life with you" to each of us. Powerful statements that allowed us to further know how they felt about us.

Powerful words spoken, undergirded by healthy relationships, create an awareness in our kids that they have a place they are from.

Looking back, my parents did not want to simply hope for the best that we got it or to mistakenly assume that because we spent time together, we would know. Powerful words spoken, undergirded by healthy relationships, create an awareness in our kids that they have a place they are from. Saying "I love doing life with you!" can be a significant comfort and calm assurance when we hear these words spoken by those we are most closely connected with and whose words can be the most influential.

Don't Want to Think About It

Our children will one day leave the home and stand on their own. You are preparing them for that moment. I know, we don't like facing that impending thought. Why can't we just enjoy the moments we have instead of dreading that fateful day? I feel it, too. Depending on the age of your kids, it's hard to even think about them ever being on their own. Enjoying our kids and family is one of the beautiful blessings that God has given parents. And preparing them to "launch" can happen in the ordinary of life that doesn't take away from enjoying them now. This preparation can add so much beauty to the moments we find ourselves in. Helping them know they have a strong sense of belonging, and where they are from, prepares them for launch down the road.

Little Habits—Big Impact

The little, ongoing, habits can also build toward something powerful for belonging that goes with your kids, and one day they will catch themselves remembering. They have no idea that this memory bank is filling with rich gold bars of memory that only gain in value as they age:

- Pizza and movie nights together on a Friday are what you do as a family.
- Driving on vacation as a family to the beach and stopping at "every" Dairy Queen.
- Setting one different dinner plate every few nights for family members. Everyone says two things they love about the person who has the special plate.

- Monday mornings are unique because everyone recites together Philippians 4:19 before the first one leaves for school.
- Dad builds a tradition by taking each kid out on a big date on their birthday. (Yes, it will continue into adulthood and get more expensive!)
- Crazy moments become a tradition when you as a parent stand and clap and yell, "Yay! You're here!" when your kids come home.
- Saturday mornings become waffle day, and everybody gets to pick their own toppings.
- When your kids start to leave the house without you, walk to the front porch to see them off.
- Every time you come home from grandparents or church, you stop and get doughnuts, and everyone gets to pick their favorite.
- And others...Unlimited memories to build!

Values Tethered to the Memories

When our kids do leave, our hope and aim is that they know where they are from—not just a place or physical house, but a tribe, a family. Our children must know they have a place they are identified, have been invited in, and included within a bond with you that is prioritized above careers, our friends, our hobbies, wants, and even the pursuit of lifestyles. When the relationship you are building with each family member, and family identity, is given precedence, each individual can know they are valued.

An interesting phenomenon occurs when relationships are strong. The values of our home—and prayerfully they are biblical values—are more likely to go with them when they are on their own. Our values are prayerfully in their hearts and minds because they are tethered to the memories, shared experiences, conversations in which we listened, encouragements we have given, and overall identity of the home they have been immersed in.

Counterfeit Message—*Imitation answers and responses the world has manufactured to satisfy the deeper needs of an individual he or she is desperate to have met.*

Counterfeits and Potential Vulnerabilities

Because of the deep need to belong or be identified with a group, our kids will look for a place to connect and a group to see as their tribe. This need is real and doesn't go away. Make sure the family is the place this need is being met first! The world has answers to this search. We know the enemy works to substitute falsehood for truth. Counterfeit messages are ever-present. The threat happens when it is activated toward, aimed at, or is pressing in on your kid. Here are three ways the world tries to coopt the need to belong being met in family:

1. *Provider vs. Cultivator*—In our attempt to build a career and lifestyle, the necessities of our family in just living life (house, cars, clothes, food, school supplies, sports teams, and more) are always in front of us. And in many cases, the ability to provide these basic living provisions can really push us to the limit. I'm referring to time, energy, and resources. That's all we can think about and try to meet. The needed time and effort it takes to meet the relational needs of our kids takes a back seat because all the other "stuff" is ever present. Our home becomes

transactional in nature and one of the core opportunities of family is not cultivated—healthy relationships and a sense of belonging.

2. *Groups of friends*—Building and nurturing friendships and a community are vital to everyone, especially kids who are learning the skills and principles of friendly bonds. But our children can easily be welcomed in by an ungodly group of friends whose friendliness can outweigh the value and biblical standards of you and your family. Your kids find themselves at a decision point of overlooking your family's values because the need to belong to a group is too great. The search and longing they feel to know they are accepted into a group doesn't stop, and if not met in the home, your kids will look in other areas.
3. *Unhealthy personal relationships*—Too often, teenagers are satisfying the need of being known and belonging through unhealthy personal/dating relationships. Depending on your kids age, these relationships can easily become emotionally unhealthy and draining. Not only do we need to tell our kids how glad we are family together, but let's also appropriately show them through hugging and physical affection.

Special Word to Fathers of Daughters

Please begin or continue to hug your daughter as she grows up. Don't pull away because you think she doesn't need it. Believe me, in certain given moments you might not be able to read her mind and emotions. Even if our words fall short, by embracing her appropriately, you sear into her mind and heart that you value your relationship with her, and you are present and with her!

4. *Social Media:* Okay parents, social media is a significant threat to your child if we are not careful. In a season of life in which they are searching for an identity, the manner they interpret likes and dislikes of their posts can lead them down a path of destructive views of themselves and their sense of worth. Many are discovering community online rather than having genuine adventures and community, and our awareness of all the dangers and developmental issues this brings is important, both for ourselves and our kids.

Let's make the home the place your kids sense belonging the most!

Uncovering the Next Layer

- What are the fresh perspectives or opportunities that come to your mind?
- Related to the need mentioned in this chapter, what are the counterfeit messages or vulnerabilities that are evident right now in your family and your kids?
- If you were being honest, what are the top obstacles that are keeping you as a parent from engaging your kids with the impact of the principles in this chapter?

Before moving on from this moment, make a list of some simple next steps you can make now:

1)

2)

3)

Chapter 8

Statement #2 "I'm Praying for You Today!"

Other ways to say it: "*You're on my mind, is there anything I can help you with or pray about?*" / "*What are three ways I can pray for you right now?*" / "*I'm praying this verse ____ over you today.*" / "*You are being watched over with love.*"

The Need Being Met: I am thought of and prayed for.

Praying for our kids and letting them know we will pray for them creates an awareness that they are valued, remembered, and lifted to the Lord throughout the day, that you as a parent value prayer, and your family will unite and lock arms together. Praying for our kids helps us live in a posture of dependence and surrender to the Lord as parents.

Preparing Our Girls for the Adventure

When our girls were younger, we lived in Lexington, Kentucky where I served for eight years in a church downtown. We had some amazing times as a family in that area with such rich memories. The winters in Kentucky during that time were especially snowy.

And when it snowed, it came down hard and really piled up. In my memory it always snowed overnight and the view out the windows in the morning was always breathtaking and otherworldly. I was ready to get out in the snow well before our girls were! Getting them prepared for the snow was a chore. The effort was labor intensive.

From putting on their multiple layers of clothing, socks, boots, gloves (if we could actually find them), hat, scarf—it was an ordeal. Of course, they always had to go to the bathroom when we got that last article of clothing on them—then we repeated the whole routine all over. The effort we had in getting them ready was a no-brainer because of the harsh elements—cold, wind, snow—that we were about to go out in. We never wondered, "Do we need to go to all this trouble?" We wanted them to be ready to confront all they were about to collide with outside and be shielded from frostbite on every appendage of their body. We knew the threat and we planned accordingly. Our tactic was to get them ready for the grand adventure outside in the dead of winter, and not to keep them inside because that was easiest or safest. Adventure awaited them! Let's get them ready to go!

I wonder if our tactics for parenting in the day to day of our homes is readying our kids for this grand venture of life. Considering the efforts we put toward getting our kids ready to play outside in the cold and snow, I wonder if we are just as adamant in getting our kids ready to confront ALL that is coming in life. I don't want to overwhelm you as a parent to the reality of all the experiences that are to come in your kids' lives. The goal is to create an awareness in us as parents to know threats are coming—along with great opportunities—and our parenting must adjust accordingly. Our kids need us to give attention, prayer, and effort to their preparation.

Praying and Readying Our Kids to Stand

If I'm unwavering that my kids wear a coat and hat outside when it's cold, I also need to think through diligently what my kids need to wear when it comes to confronting a spiritual adversary that is going to attack and attempt to thwart any plans for spiritual growth. In Ephesians 6:10–21, Paul challenged us as followers of Christ to be ready to stand in the midst of the devil's attacks that will come. What if we approach our parenting with this in mind?

Three Principles We Can Learn From This Passage as We Lead Our Kids

- **Depend on Him alone—not our own strength.**

Our strategies and planning in parenting with intention ultimately fall short without the Lord, because our battle is not against flesh but the spiritual realm. We need Him! Let's remember, the purpose of family is NOT to present a "snow globe" family to others in which we all just look good in an Instagram picture. There is nothing wrong with having a beautiful family and great pictures; just don't stop with that commitment. The purpose is ultimately about Him and our family's becoming a launching pad for our kids to make known the mystery of the gospel wherever life takes them.

- **The suit of spiritual armor is fitted for movement.**

Lead and pray for your kids to stand when confronted with trials and advance. As a parent, our goal is not simply to have our kids develop a defensive stance, but an offensive posture for the gospel. Like a track runner's stance that is eager and equipped to move forward, may our family be standing at the starting line ready to go!

Let's evaluate the indicators of the spiritual health of our kids. Are we satisfied when our kids "don't sin" in certain situations or content to applaud what they didn't do? Might our goal become spurring them on toward a confidence in which they share the gospel? Our goal can't simply be sin prevention or sin management in our kids. The overall hope is that our kids understand whose they are and then choose to engage the world with the truth of Christ.

- **View the family as a cohort.**

Situations arise in which we must lock arms or shields with others we trust deeply to defend or move forward in community. Lead your family to be a cohort for each other. As a part of locking arms together, Paul highlighted the necessity of believers praying and then he encouraged others to pray for him.

Praying for and Standing With Your Kids

Let's unpack this a little more and the impact of Paul's request found in Ephesians 6:19. How might this appeal for prayer impact our view and role as parents today?

> Pray also for me, that the message may be given to me when I open my mouth to make known with boldness the mystery of the gospel (Ephesians 6:19).

In verse 19, the Apostle Paul asked the church in Ephesus to pray for him. And what a prayer it was! He asked this group of believers to stand in the gap with him and pray that he would have boldness and clarity of words in proclaiming the mystery of the gospel when He spoke. I've often been encouraged and challenged by Paul's request here. Paul was the foremost and greatest evangelist for the gospel, and he asked for prayer.

Paul desired to get others not only to pray for him, but he wanted them to know the specific things that he needed prayer for. Not only does God want His people to pray, but I'm sure Paul gained remarkable confidence knowing that others were with him in prayer. He knew he had others locking arms with him in prayer. He wrote in Philemon 1:7 and 2 Timothy 1:16 of finding encouragement and joy from believers who refresh him in his times of need. Lean into meeting this same need for your kids that Paul had in specific times of his life when others encouraged him. Let our kids know we are praying for them!

Whether our kids are beginning to feel pressures and threats for the first time, or they have been in the thick of things many times, let's let them know we are standing with them. Yes, depending on the ages of our kids, they might think we are just prying and interfering in their lives. Or they may be at the age of seeking independence and want to show you they already know everything there is to know in life and are just fine without you. (This is when you can chuckle on the inside.) Remember, we must look past the visible, veneer thick, and above the smirk or attitude they might give us in the moment to their deeper needs.

There is a big need in the mind and heart of our kids that is waiting to be met, a need for them to know you are praying for them and thinking about what they must deal with. As the Apostle Paul was encouraged to know that he had prayer warriors, may our kids hear the words from us and know. For many of us, prayer remains an idea or an aspiration. Let's move it to a practice in our lives as parents and let the family know we trust and are dependent upon a

Let's move it to a practice in our lives as parents and let the family know we trust and are dependent upon a holy God.

holy God. We are outfitting them in spiritual clothes for the battle ahead. And we want to know the specifics of their requests as they venture out. Adventure awaits! Let's get them ready to go!

Five Areas of Focus to Pray for Our Kids

1. Tender hearts that are sensitive to God's leading.
2. Courage to stand for what's right, even if they are the only ones.
3. Pray the prayer for our kids that Paul asked for himself in Ephesians 6:19.
4. Craving for God's Word and a thirst for time with Him.
5. Begin the pattern of understanding Sabbath with the Lord.

What if we trust God more in the way we pray for our kids? He is God—let's entrust our kids to Him!

Counterfeits and Vulnerabilities

When we are challenged or compelled to pray, let's be aware of counterfeit responses that could exist in our hearts and minds, and ways we might be vulnerable to listen to the lies of an enemy that wants to destroy our families.

- We don't feel spiritual enough to pray or haven't earned that right.

- We don't believe our prayers are effective, so we don't pray.
- We pray cautious prayers. We don't pray big and risky prayers that seem too vast, so we keep them small and within reach (in our opinion) for God.
- We are conditioned to receive immediate answers or responses to our needs. We might not find patience to wait on an answer from God.
- I believe many of us find ourselves nervous about the response or answer God might give to our prayers that we have not planned for. We think it's just better not to pray in order to "be safe."
    - What if God is moving in a direction in the hearts of our kids that goes against our plan for them?
    - What if the answer is out of our comfort zone?
- We don't understand there is a real adversary that is seeking to defeat the minds and hearts of our kids.
- We need to be mindful not to flippantly say we will pray for them. If not careful, this is a statement that says we simply care, instead of lifting them up in prayer to the Father.
- We can believe we've done enough in preparing them in our own strategy and strength without looking to Scripture for guidance.

Let's make the home the place your kids know they are prayed for the most!

Uncovering the Next Layer

1. What are the fresh perspectives or opportunities that come to your mind?

2. Related to the need mentioned in this chapter, what are the counterfeit messages or vulnerabilities that are evident right now in your family and kids?
3. If you were being honest, what are the top obstacles that are keeping you as a parent from engaging your kids with the impact of the principles in this chapter?

Before moving on from this moment, make a list of some simple next steps you can make now:

1)

2)

3)

Chapter 9

STATEMENT #3
"I BELIEVE IN YOU!"

Other ways to say it: *"I have confidence in you."* / *"I know I've been correcting you a lot lately, but please know that never changes how much I love you and believe in you."* / *"You can do it!"*/ *"Yes! I knew you could do it!"* / *"I'm such a fan of all God is doing in your life."* / *"You used the wisdom I know you have well."*

The Need Being Met:
Someone believes in me and trusts in me.

Noticing the Shifts That Are Occurring

As our children grow and figure out how to navigate new things for the first time, we have daily opportunities to encourage and help them to know how to do simple tasks and succeed in doing them. It might have been helping them sit up for the first time when they were babies, as they started walking, riding a bike, or even learning basic school subjects. What a blessing to play a part in those milestones.

Yes, we might find ourselves getting a little frustrated along the way because our patience sometimes runs thin, but when they "get it," we all burst with excitement. When my daughters played sports, whatever the skill set that needed to be refined, I enjoyed encouraging and coaching in areas that I knew, but I absolutely loved to shout out, “I knew you could do it! Yes!” when they achieved doing the skill. Those little moments along their journey, built confidence in their minds and hearts and served as permission for them to continue moving forward.

Like the awareness we have of basic tasks our kids reach, I believe it is vital we notice the shifts that are occurring in our kids in areas of responsibility. Are these times messy, unpleasant, exciting, disorderly, enjoyable, frustrating, fun, and chaotic? Yep! In those early years, we easily communicate belief in our kids as every milestone brings a celebration. But especially during adolescence, they are grappling with an increasing awkwardness. They’re feeling so inept as they clumsily navigate in so many areas of their lives that are all brand new to them. If we could see inside their thoughts, we might see that they feel as if they are stepping onto a football field with snorkeling flippers, a fishing rod, and a spoon. Though they may not ask for us to tell them during these years, regularly communicating our belief in them is crucial.

New emotions that constantly change are coming out of nowhere, while their friends are all shifting in their own emotions and at different levels. Many kids feel for the first time like they’re equally too much and not enough—at the same time. They begin to think they have to start proving themselves worthy, even though they don’t even know why or to what standards they are trying to reach. They don’t feel social or emotional permission to make mistakes. Even though they

When we verbalize our confidence in them, they can borrow that confidence when they don’t yet feel their own.

are still incredibly dependent upon us, they are desperate to show they are independent. And amid all of this, many are beginning to sense the convictions of the Holy Spirit in their lives as biblical truths are impressed on them. These are the moments we must be alert for to encourage and coach them—and yes, we will probably get frustrated along the way. But when they "get it," we shout out, "Yes! I knew you could do it!" When we verbalize our confidence in them, they can borrow that confidence when they don't yet feel their own.

Wrestling and Learning Lab

As parents, we have the privilege of a front row seat to observing our children wrestle with applying truth to everyday decisions. As a parent, you are chosen by God in His design to be present as they are adopting truth they know in their head. Truth moves from head knowledge into their heart and then into situations lived out… most likely not perfectly. But these moments are pivotal points in their life that allow them to begin to experience major shifts in independence and responsibility. While still under the cover of the home's safeguard, a learning lab takes place. In simple terms, they are learning how to walk for the first time in all types of situations.

These moments aren't only imminent, they are necessary in owning one's faith. Be aware of these times that are coming and encourage your children as they navigate these decisions. Remember, we have many more years of experience than they do in figuring out how to live life in obedience to the Lord, and if we are honest, we still find ourselves falling short along the way. We, too, have had others who have been on the sideline in our lives shouting words of encouragement that they believed in us, even in moments when we didn't believe in ourselves.

Let Them Know You're Not Going Anywhere

The beauty of your child knowing you have confidence in them is powerful. Speak the words "I believe in you!" so they hear it from you. While this will certainly be connected to levels of trust in your home, consider trustworthy patterns, no matter how small, that can be acknowledged. Situations will arise and moments are coming that your child will believe he or she can never do anything right and is simply a mistake. They will at times feel alone and isolated with nowhere to go. Build toward a healthy relationship that serves as a safety net to this thinking and let them know you aren't going anywhere. Have a resolve that you are the one who is present, available, and the one to speak assurance into their lives when they feel isolated. When they are vulnerable to listening to the lies they are telling themselves, start responding with truth, grace, and mercy.

Now, are there times to discipline, correct, and for them to receive consequences? Yes. But these components are not intended as the end result. Can these times allow us to speak into their need for the gospel because of sin? Yes! If conviction is falling like rain on their hearts, lead them to the rescue and reconciliation that Christ brings by placing faith in Him. These also become moments to respond with grace and mercy, no matter how complicated and messy. Those moments of messing up ultimately don't define who they are, and we need to make sure how they view themselves is not tethered to those mistakes.

As a follower of Christ, we should understand this truth of living under grace by faith and being set free from doing in order to receive His love. We get to walk in grace and mercy every day knowing the freedom we have by living without the bondage to the law. Phew! So, let's be challenged and encouraged to make every decision and action of our parenting driven by the gospel, not by the laws of religion. Here's a quote I came across a few years ago that describes my hope and passion in how I relate with my daughters, sons-in-law, and now grandkids.

RELIGION – "I messed up. Dad's gonna kill me."

GOSPEL – "I messed up. I need to call dad."

–Jeremy Rose, Axis Church of Nashville

This need to know that someone is available, caring, and believes in us is real and doesn't go away. Lead and relate in a way that the family is the place where this need is being met by speaking words that encourages and spurs them on!

Counterfeits and Vulnerabilities

The following are two counterfeit messages and lies that your kids might be vulnerable to. Included are some assumptions that they also can draw conclusions from when they sense no one believes in them:

1. Kids feel they are a mistake and can't do anything right.

When they feel no one believes in them, kids can't get over the hump of believing they are a failure, and their confidence and assurance continues to be torn down by further mistakes they make. Situations will arise and moments are coming that kids will believe he or she can never do anything right. Yes, these include lapses in judgments, moments of disrespect, or a complete lack of obedience. The way we respond, and the words we say can speak to layers of identity and how they view themselves. We don't want them to build a false narrative that they are a mistake. They are just someone who makes mistakes. Even in our best efforts to do what's right as parents, we can all fall short ourselves in how we respond in certain situations. Here is the beauty—let's also apply grace and mercy to our parenting and let's reconcile with our kids in those times we say things we don't mean.

2. **Kids can feel isolated and alone thinking they have nowhere to go.**

When our kids make bad decisions or mistakes, they could feel alone and isolated with nowhere to go. Let's make sure that our unrealistic expectations are not the primary source of the pressure they are feeling. This is another area that I heard from many students through the years when I was a student minister—the relentless burden they felt from their parents to succeed with little room to learn and grow. To be fair to every parent out there, our kids may have "unrealistic expectations" when we ask them to do a common chore. My wife and I lived through those early years when our daughters felt like Cinderella because we asked them to simply keep their dirty clothes from piling up on the floor of their room. When they know we believe in them no matter what, they have a better baseline for interpreting feelings of failure and isolation. My encouragement for you is to be constant in your observation of how approachable you are and assessing the words you speak. Seek understanding, forgiveness, unity, and restoration!

Let's make the home the place your kids sense being believed in the most!

Uncovering the Next Layer

- What are the fresh perspectives or opportunities that come to your mind?

- Related to the need mentioned in this chapter, what are the counterfeit messages or vulnerabilities that are evident right now in your family and kids?
- If you were being honest, what are the top obstacles that are keeping you as a parent from engaging your kids with the impact of the principles in this chapter?

Before moving on from this moment, make a list of some simple next steps you can make now:

1)

2)

3)

Chapter 10

Statement #4 "True Life Is Found in Christ!"

Other ways to say it: *"Jesus loves you—follow Him!"* / *"You have purpose and value because He says you do!"* / *"You can trust Him."* / *"Your identity is found in who Christ says you are!"*

The Need Being Met: Salvation, Identity, Purpose

Everyone needs a Savior from his or her sin. Only Christ can rescue us by His death, burial, and resurrection. By His grace, through faith in Christ, we can be saved. No matter the age, every person is striving to find the answers that quench the search for significance and identity. The gospel fills this longing and void. Christ is the only one who can ultimately meet this need. Let them hear it from you!

Salvation Story

The privilege we have as parents to share the greatest truth of all with our kids still astounds me. God, in His infinite wisdom, has handed to the parents the primary responsibility to pass on the story of God to the next generation. We see it in Psalms 78:1–7 that we are to teach our children so they will know of His story with the hope they will put their trust in Him.

We are to specifically share the salvation message with our kids. Does the church have a role in this? Absolutely! But Matthew 28:19–20 is directed to parents also and should lead out in shaping the course of our parenting. The family is designed to be a place that not only lives out the gospel, but along with the church, the home is to clearly communicate the good news of Jesus to our kids. Our role as parents is to let our kids know of their sin condition and that the only remedy is to follow Jesus. This includes leading our children to understand and embrace the Lord, teaching repentance (turning away from sin), and praying for them to have a renewed heart from the impact of sin by saying yes to Him. Let's have conversations about it with them! When we are tuned in, we see lots of opportunities from the time our kids are small to lay the groundwork for the gospel by talking about God's love and His character.

Our role as parents is to let our kids know of their sin condition and that the only remedy is to follow Jesus.

As we are called to be disciples who make disciples, let's turn our attention to our kids. All humans, including our children, will be active at some point to pursue meaning, purpose, and significance in their lives. Maybe especially in this time, kids feel desperate to attach their lives to something that is bigger than them. Let's use words that clearly communicate to our kids our desire for them to run toward Christ to meet those needs! May our kids place their salvation, hope, and identity in Him—turning our focus toward leading our kids to become active followers of Christ versus passive believers. Methods and specifics of how we disciple our kids change as they grow, but we are called to always keep encouraging their spiritual growth as a primary goal.

Our Identity

My grandad had a lake house just 20 minutes from my home growing up, so to say the least, we were at his house a lot. Around age 8, I was eager to learn boating skills and could not wait to be old enough to take the ski boat out. In the meantime, my granddad let me take the canoe out, and often by myself. Just one catch though, when I took it out by myself, he would tie one end of an extra-long ski rope to the back of the canoe and the other end of the rope to a large oak tree that stood firm on the lake shore.

It is amazing looking back on those days in that canoe when I felt so much freedom, yet I was still tied to a tree and could only go so far. Freedom found in being tied down, that seems paradoxical. As I paddled out in the lake, I knew the rope would eventually tighten, and the currents of water could not pull me away. Freedom came from having confidence in knowing that whatever I lacked in my ability to paddle and navigate that canoe, I was secure because I was tethered to that tree.

Understanding the truth that as followers of Jesus Christ, our identity is tied to Christ and who He says we are, is like that rope tied to that oak tree on the lakeshore. No matter what we face or circumstances we encounter, we know that all is secure in Him. This truth is vital for our kids to understand when they become believers and followers of Him. As they grow in Him, as we live out the gospel in front of them, and as we speak truth into their lives, our kids become more and more assured of how they are tethered to who

Jesus says they are. When Jesus, the way He has saved us, the ways He is saving us, and the ways He will save us are all part of our regular conversations and celebrations, we are making Him central in our family life.

Understanding Purpose: When someone truly hears the gospel of Christ, surrenders their life to Him, and allows the Lord, through His Spirit and Word to transform them, everything begins to change.

- A persons' purpose in life is discovered and why they were created awakens.
- Perspective of how one views school, friends, career, family, community, and money changes. If we are here because of Him and to make Him known, then everything is seen through that viewpoint.

Two Encouragements to Help Our Kids Grow

1. The Bible Is God's Living Word

Our kids need to know and observe that we value the Bible, and we read it and build our lives around its truths. As we study it, our identity is built on the truths of who Christ is! Let them see you reading and studying His Word.

- **Isaiah 55:8–11**

  "For my thoughts are not your thoughts, and your ways are not my ways." This is the Lord's declaration. "For as heaven is higher than earth, so my ways are higher than your ways, and my thoughts than your thoughts. For just as rain and snow fall from heaven and do not return there without saturating the earth and making it germinate and sprout, and providing seed to sow and food to eat, so my word that comes from my mouth will not return to me empty, but it will accomplish what I please and will prosper in what I send it to do."

- **Hebrews 4:12**

  For the word of God is living and effective and sharper than any double-edged sword, penetrating as far as the separation of soul and spirit, joints and marrow. It is able to judge the thoughts and intentions of the heart.

2. The Church Is a Biblical Community

The church is a local body of believers where our family will hear and experience biblical truths alongside others. There is beauty in engaging in the entirety of the church as family—in corporate worship, small group biblical community, praying, tithing (and modeling to our kids that they can bring their tithe), growing alongside others, missional experiences, working through disagreement or conflict, and serving others. When we build in the discipline of consistently being engaged as a family with our church family, we are all helped in building identity as followers of Christ.

- **Hebrews 10:24–25**

  And let us consider one another in order to provoke love and good works, not neglecting to gather together, as some are in the habit of doing, but encouraging each other, and all the more as you see the day approaching.

- **Acts 2:42**

  They devoted themselves to the apostles' teaching, to the fellowship, to the breaking of bread, and to prayer.

Counterfeits and Vulnerabilities

- Everyone will strive for significance and identity, and if not found in Christ, the search will lead them to what this world has to offer. The search doesn't stop.
- Crafty lies about God, Christ, the church, and the Bible will come in many forms. Sound understanding and experience in truth helps us (and our kids) be less susceptible to them.
- Identity might be found temporarily in accomplishments or even how well we succeed (sports, job, school, band, etc.), what we own (car, clothes, phone, etc.), or even from the applause of people, groups of friends, or community—online or in person. All of these accomplishments fall short and are temporary.
- We may be lulled into believing we don't really need Scripture. (Really a form of pride.) The Bible can become simply an option—and is relegated to church, not our everyday lives. The Bible can be seen as outdated and not relevant to our lives today.
- The reality of sin and our need for salvation is not emphasized. If we were to stop for a moment and write on a whiteboard the top ten things we need to direct our parenting toward, I would think that His message of salvation would be number one.
- Jesus becomes something we simply accommodate into our home instead of making Him the banner of our family's distinctiveness. We tend to pacify the longings of our heart by giving lip service to the Creator of life and His message of redemption. Our kids pick up on this and what our actions are shouting.

Let's make the home the place your kids hear the gospel the most!

Uncovering the Next Layer

- What are the fresh perspectives or opportunities that come to your mind?
- Related to the need mentioned in this chapter, what are the counterfeit messages or vulnerabilities that are evident right now in your family and kids?
- If you were being honest, what are the top obstacles that are keeping you as a parent from engaging your kids with the impact of the principles in this chapter?

Before moving on from this moment, make a list of some simple next steps you can make now:

1)

2)

3)

Chapter 11

Statement #5 "I've Got Your Back!"

Other ways to say it: *"I see you." / "I will defend you!"/ "I need you to know that you are not alone." / "I'm sorry you are going through this, let's tackle this together." / "You can lean on me for strength."*

The Need Being Met:
I am seen and have an advocate on my side.

We need to know that we are seen, someone is in our corner as our advocate; someone will show up when we become desperate who is looking out for what's best for us. This need is real and doesn't go away.

The Unseen Work of a Bridge Beam

A beautiful river near our home in Tennessee provides an enchanted waterway for my wife and I to get on our kayaks and paddle our way down. It's not a big river but just the right width as it winds its way through the small downtown area we live near. As you make your way downstream you take an amazing journey below the overhanging trees and rock cliffs that make up most of its shoreline. As you float, you occasionally travel below several bridges for highways that make their way into the downtown area.

From under the bridges, you can see the beams that span the width of the river and connect to the concrete pylons that are buried deep into the banks of the hillside by the river. Even if the currents of the river might be stronger under these bridges, it's usually strangely quiet and serene, as you observe the sounds of cars above driving across and people walking over. I'm always intrigued by the exertion that those beams provide without any notice from above. They do the work, which they were designed to do; they bare the weight of the cars, trucks, and people who walk, run, or bike across. I realize that happens all over the world across thousands of bridges with beams made up of either wood, concrete, or steel. But when you are on the river, looking up at the beams as they carry this massive load without any recognition, you can't help but pause and ponder.

What a picture of a role parents can fulfill in the lives of our kids! We want to let them know they are not alone. As we are in relationship with them, we get to hear the pulse of their lives and be tuned into some of the trials they might be going through. Remember, the emotions they are feeling, no matter how small to us, are very real and large to them. Every child will be confronted with varying degrees of moments of feeling isolated, sensing enormous pressure to be accepted, feeling like a failure, or listening to lies they aren't enough.

Depending on the age of your child, they are in the early stages of figuring it out because these feelings are new. Many might think they are the only ones going through these pressures. Let them know they are not alone as they desperately search for pylons on the bank shore to find stability. We might be "below and out of sight," but they know we are fully accessible. As parents, we can speak powerful words into their hearts to let them know they are seen and that we have their back. As the beams help carry the weight, you as a parent will stand in the gap when they feel overwhelmed.

Yes, we must approach these moments with discernment on how much to carry for them. Natural consequences can be a wonderful teacher, and they need to learn problem solving and relational skills independently. Our goal is not just to protect them, but to prepare them for a life lived to the fullest for God. But preparation doesn't mean allowing them to wander alone trying to figure it out by themselves in those dark times. Trial and error works best to some degree when a safety net is present. A strong relationship is that appropriate safety net, which can serve as a backdrop or beam that can help carry them. They know it's there, and that is a huge step. And as we appropriately figure out the weight they need to carry, we can use our words to encourage and confidently let them know we will show up. The beam we can serve as, is to build in them an assurance that they are not alone. We're there and in their corner.

> **As parents, we can speak powerful words into their hearts to let them know they are seen and that we have their back.**

Bella and Curtis' Story

"He showed up!" That's the phrase that really grabbed my attention when I sat down with Bella to hear some of her story. We were on a mission trip to Chicago with a team of students and adults, and I was planning to have a quick conversation with her about something back home. Bella was a 17-year-old and active in our church. Her dad, Curtis, was also on the trip with us, and I had observed their close relationship. Before I got up from our conversation, I wanted her to know that I loved watching their father-daughter relationship play out and had taken notice. Just a quick word of encouragement—that's what I thought.

She said a few things about her dad, then started sharing about her middle school years, being bullied and feeling alone during that time. Skimming through this massive story of her life, she shared that her dad was home during those years, but always busy as he built a business. Then jumping to a porch conversation she had with her dad, she shared that they both opened their hearts to each other in a new way. "I didn't know he had a similar story as mine, and I was so encouraged," she said. He made the statement, "Bella, I'm in your corner!" From that point on, she said, "he showed up!" From that conversation, she knew, "he had my back."

As she shared critical parts of her story, it was obvious there was a lot behind those two phrases. I sat there and asked, "I need to hear more about this, can you go back to what you just said?" I asked her if she felt comfortable unpacking those phrases, she just used, "he showed up and he had my back." She smiled really big and talked openly about the turn that took place in their relationship. These immense feelings and needs that she was carrying alone were now beginning to be met by her father in a deep way. Needs such as "I felt alone," "I thought nobody cared," and "I have nobody to go to about how I feel" were now in the open with her dad. She felt like he began to see her in a new way, and he was now choosing time with her over his business. He began to listen and showed that he cared. "He asked questions about my 'whole life' and was intent on learning about my friends."

After that powerful conversation, I had to go straight to her dad. "Curtis, I just had the best conversation with Bella. You need to know how much I loved hearing about your relationship with her." I had this strong desire to thank him for his intentionality. To not only recognize his daughters' needs but his decision to step into his role as a parent. I blindsided him with such an affirmation and his eyes quickly filled with tears.

I sat down with them both a few weeks later to take a deeper dive into their relationship. Curtis shared more of the changes that he began to make and the clarity that he had discovered over the years. He called that time in his life, his "epiphany of priorities."

Here are some of his thoughts on how he sees these priorities impacting his intentionality with Bella:

- This "epiphany of priorities" sets the course for all other choices in my relationship with my only daughter. All forthcoming decisions cascade from this pivotal choice, "love the Lord above all, and then be a husband and father."
- I had to set my values; everything comes from that.
- I knew it was essential to be a parent to her before being a friend.
- I have discovered that I need to be open and share appropriately what has happened in my life. I needed to model honesty, and that I'm not too big that things don't happen to me even now.
- I discovered that my relationship with my daughter is a platform for doing life with her. The health of that relationship allows me to know my daughter. It builds a deeper trust between us to have ongoing honest conversations.

- I had to move from being just a provider in her life and toward building a relationship.
- I had to redefine with her that when I was home, she knew I was with her. Earlier in my parenting, I might have been physically in the room, but I wasn't there mentally or emotionally. I began to realize this shift needed to occur of shutting down my work to relate with her. My role as a father is of the utmost importance.
- I ask this question to myself quite often: How can I better relate to her? I'm always looking for and finding areas.

Curtis became aware of how he was relating to Bella and then made an intentional pivot to connect with her in a new way. This should challenge all of us. He took notice and became dissatisfied with how he was meeting her needs and changed course. He didn't just make excuses or cast blame on someone or something else. The decisions he needed to make had a cost in other areas, and he was willing to pay it because of the value he now placed on his relationship with his daughter, which brought with it the greatest of rewards.

The Posture of a Shepherd

> How happy is the one who does not walk in the advice of the wicked or stand in the pathway with sinners or sit in the company of mockers! Instead, his delight is in the LORD's instruction, and he meditates on it day and night. He is like a tree planted beside flowing streams that bears its fruit in its season, and its leaf does not wither. Whatever he does prospers (Psalm 1:1–3).

Many years ago, I heard an illustration about the posture a shepherd knows to take when he himself drinks water. It's not just the sheep that are to drink and hydrate to stay healthy. The shepherd kneels next to the stream, scoops water with his hands bringing the water up to his mouth, and keeps his eyes on the landscape the whole time. All the while being observant to any threats as he drinks.

He wouldn't dare lap the water with his mouth while bent over with his face on the water because this action leaves him vulnerable. As he drinks the water, he is always watching with his eyes on the sheep while attentive to any wild animals. He is alert, on guard, and vigilant to the dangers that could be lurking. The shepherd is aware of how vulnerable the sheep are when they are exposed. He knows his role, his focus, and has prepared for what he might be up against to defend himself and his flock of sheep.

> My God, my rock, in whom I take refuge. My shield, the horn of my salvation, my stronghold, my refuge, and my Savior, you save me from violence (2 Samuel 22:3).

As we parent each of our kids, we must take care of our souls and "drink" deeply from His streams of living water ourselves, staying spiritually and emotionally healthy. It's in these moments as we study and live out God's Word that we grow in overall fellowship and understanding of the Lord.

As we do this, may we remain diligent in always looking for any threats and areas of vulnerabilities our kids are susceptible to. Many influences of this world can distract us and keep our attention away from our kids. It's in those moments of distraction that the enemy can slither his way in and cause havoc in the minds and hearts of our kids. Distractions can also interrupt our understanding of what we are to be looking for by way of threats.

Do you know the threats and vulnerabilities of your kids? Areas our kids might be susceptible can come in many forms and may not always be visible to us. Threats don't just walk into the family living area and tell us they are here. As parents let's understand our role, be diligent in observing any threats or vulnerabilities out there and learn how to identify them as we prepare ourselves for what we might be up against.

Counterfeits and Vulnerabilities

- Quite often, our children will feel alone and as though they are facing life's obstacles on their own (bullying, pressure they put on themselves, parents' expectations! (ouch)). Feeling isolated can often lead them down a somewhat risky path where they are pressed with finding a way out on their own.
- Although kids need to be able to work through situations that have consequences and understand problem solving, the family can be a safe place for trial and errors of life to be made. Therefore, the framework of family provides a safety net, a backdrop for gained wisdom, and a place for supportive and restorative conversations to occur.
- Lies they are hearing from others:
    - You need to be like everyone else.
    - Your worth and identity are tied to what you do.
- Lies they are telling themselves:
    - I'm too much.
    - I'm not enough.

- You need to figure it out all by yourself.
- If you shared what's on your heart, no one would understand.
- You're the only one that thinks that way.

Becoming aware of lies our kids are believing takes attending, listening, and discernment, all bathed in prayer. Sometimes God shows us plainly, and sometimes we must trust He is working where we can't see. As we prepare and defend them, instill biblical truth into their hearts and minds so the Scriptures will provide a true response to all the counterfeits, vulnerabilities, and lies listed above.

Let's make the home the place your kids sense they are defended the most!

Uncovering the Next Layer

- What are the fresh perspectives or opportunities that come to your mind?
- Related to the need mentioned in this chapter, what are the counterfeit messages or vulnerabilities that are evident right now in your family and kids?
- If you were being honest, what are the top obstacles that are keeping you as a parent from engaging your kids with the impact of the principles in this chapter?

Before moving on from this moment, make a list of some simple next steps you can make now:

1)

2)

3)

Chapter 12

Statement #6 "*I Forgive You!*"

Other ways to say it: "*You are always welcome here.*" / "*You always have a place here.*"/ "*I look forward to seeing you!*" / "*We're going to move forward!*"

The Need Being Met: I can be forgiven, and I am longed for. There's hope after I make a mistake.

The fear of messing up or failure is real. To know we are longed for by others, even though we let others down in how we act or decisions we have made, can give an assurance to our identity. May we model reconciliation and let our kids know their mistakes do not define them.

Allowing God to Work on Our Heart

Let's be honest with this statement. We might find ourselves in a situation these words can be tough to verbalize to our own kids right now. Or even harder to really mean it. We might be in a season—or one might be on the horizon—when we are really wrestling with God on this one. To release someone from the expectation that they can fix whatever harm they have caused us or others can be a major obstacle. From being hurt emotionally by what our kids said to us, embarrassed by their actions in public, or discovering their actions of flat-out disobedience to what we expect of them, we are caught in a vortex of emotions that can be massive burdens on our minds and hearts.

We have the clear picture laid out before us that we are to take to move forward. Will it be easy? It's probably contingent on the infraction we feel we have received. But here's the truth.

Forgiveness that is given by grace, through faith in Christ, is a pillar of our Christian doctrine. Those of us who are followers of Christ have eagerly come to Him in acknowledgment of our sin, in repentance and faith, and therefore are reconciled in relationship with the God of all creation. Our sins are forgiven and are wiped clean. This is an acceptance of a gift that we did not earn.

> In him we have redemption through his blood, the forgiveness of our trespasses, according to the riches of his grace that he richly poured out on us with all wisdom and understanding (Ephesians 1:7–8).

As we place our trust in Christ's work on the cross and His resurrection, the reality of shame, guilt, failure, and condemnation are lifted and gone. The sense of feeling the weight of those things needs to vanish from our mind and heart also. Forgiveness means the erasure of those burdens. We celebrate that truth that has been applied to us and in turn lived out through our interactions with others, including being kind and forgiving when someone wrongs us.

> And be kind and compassionate to one another, forgiving one another, just as God also forgave you in Christ (Ephesians 4:32).

Three Steps to Take to Restore One's Heart When We Think We Can't Forgive

1. Sit with God in silence. His ability to speak truth and conviction into the crevices of our lives when we are silent before Him is difficult and yet freedom can be found in those times.
2. Let's examine our heart considering Jesus' approach to forgiveness. We are recipients of His great forgiveness that we did not deserve.
3. Let's confess it to God. Be honest with Him—He already knows how you feel. Agree with what He already knows. Release and accept!

Forgiveness and the Remarkable Effect of Reconciliation

The reason we forgive others is not based on attempting to gain forgiveness and salvation; we forgive others because we are forgiven by God. We are moved because of His love and forgiveness. Let that move us to have compassion for others, especially in the relationships of family. It's in this place of closeness and knowledge of each other's struggles and weaknesses that forgiveness can resonate the most. Forgive, forget, and release the expectation that our family members can fix it.

When parents verbally let their kids know they are forgiven, the heart of the gospel is demonstrated. Those times our kids mess up and know they have failed in front of us can lead to shame and guilt. As the Spirit works on their heart and they are moved to repentance, let's recognize those moments and lean into guiding them through

When parents verbally let their kids know they are forgiven, the heart of the gospel is on full display.

these rough waters. We have an opportunity to reconcile with them and let them know their mistakes do not define them. Freedom is not only found in these moments but also felt the most.

This is where the beautiful picture can be shown of the gospel being given to us and not gained by our efforts. We can lead our kids toward understanding the ultimate forgiveness that Jesus gives through repentance—not forcing the gospel on them or being led by legalism through unrealistic expectations. Let them know through words and the strength of relationship that being welcomed into one's family is gifted and not gained by how we present ourselves or effort. And forgiving each other is a marker of being in family together.

Counterfeits and Vulnerabilities

1. Kids will go where they are welcomed no matter what—and too often it's the "world" that has wide open arms to receive them as they are. Because Christ's call to obedience and biblical standards aren't present in the world, the sense of judgment or conviction isn't present. These are those moments we forgive and embrace our kids while encouraging them toward Christ's love, which brings reconciliation and purpose.
2. We often will sit in a place of judgment at home because we know each other so well. Seeking reconciliation and moving forward with forgiveness must be hallmarks of our families.

Be careful not to weaponize past blunders and mistakes our kids have made when we are irritated. Phrases like "you always" and "why can't you ever do anything right?" paint a description on their mind and heart that they are defined by their actions.

3. We are tempted to "sweep it under the rug" when dealing with being wronged or embarrassed because we either want harmony or don't want to deal with it. We must forgive in those moments and work through our emotions. The side effect is that one's reactions build up and are predisposed to come out in anger.
4. This need is real and doesn't go away. Make sure the family is the place of being forgiven and fully welcomed in is being met!

Our Opportunity in Asking Our Kids for Forgiveness

Statement: *"I'm sorry. I apologize, will you forgive me?"*

Need to be met: For your child to know that we all need forgiveness. That we can forgive others, and for them to know we all make mistakes, and that the relationship can be redeemed and restored.

I believe one of the lies we tell ourselves as parents is that we can't fail in front of our kids. Either we think we must be seen like we have it all together or we need to put up a front as though we have no faults. And we can easily fall into this trap when it comes to not letting our kids know when we might be wrong or have missed it in a parenting decision we have made. Maybe it was a mistaken conclusion we made on reading a situation we saw them in or the way we blew up emotionally at them on a day when other areas of our life were causing stress. It's hard to admit we were wrong, and it's in those times we can hurt them emotionally.

In this pivotal moment we feel convicted and know in our spirit we messed up; we are presented with two primary options. One is to double down on our stubbornness and build a false narrative that closes the possibility of connection with our kids to get to the other side of the issue. Or we can embrace humility and honesty in that moment that places you and your child on common ground that brings about restoration and a depth to your relationship. We must choose the option of vulnerability with them in the mess and ask for forgiveness. The power of this action reverberates out to impact all areas of a relationship, especially in the context of a parent and child relationship.

An Example of Forgiveness From My Father

One of those moments of being asked for forgiveness from me is with my dad when I was around nine years old. My dad came to my room after an incident to tell me he was wrong in how he acted and asked for forgiveness. That was a long, long time ago, but it has been etched in my mind ever since and became a cornerstone conversation that deepened my relationship with him.

He had asked me to help him remove a bench seat out of our family van. He had loosened all the bolts and fasteners but needed help getting it out. As I was in the van to assist, I scooted the seat instead of lifting it. It tore a big gash in the carpet. "What did you do that for?!?" he shouted! It startled me and I pushed the bench seat back and tore the carpet even more. "Linc, lift the seat, son!" Without saying another word, we finally got it out and put it where it needed to go in the basement. I slipped away to my room and just sat on the edge of my bed bewildered and hurt by what just happened. My dad never loses it like that, and I really felt isolated.

In about ten minutes, he knocked on my door and asked if he could come in. I said yes and he came in and sat next to me. He told me he messed up with no excuses. He said, "Linc, I'm sorry for hurting you. Can you forgive me?" I couldn't talk but said yes by hugging my father. My father modeled to me then, and at other times, the power of seeking forgiveness and owning when he knew he fell short. What might appear simple and unassuming today was a life-giving moment for a nine-year-old that was out of fellowship with his father and was now restored.

Saying these words can be a significant comfort and assurance when we as parents own the moments and situations where we have blown it. If we aren't honest, we can perpetuate the lie of perfectionism and undermine the perception of our need for grace. To acknowledge the fact that we related incorrectly with our kids or admit that we made decisions in haste and our mistaken choices impacted them in a negative manner has enormous impact on us and our children. May we each be honest with our kids and seek forgiveness just as our desire for them to come to us. You can do it!

Saying these words can be a significant comfort and assurance when we as parents own the moments and situations where we have blown it.

Let's make the home the place your kids know forgiveness the most!

Uncovering the Next Layer

- What are the fresh perspectives or opportunities that come to your mind?
- Related to the need mentioned in this chapter, what are the counterfeit messages or vulnerabilities that are evident right now in your family and kids?
- If you were being honest, what are the top obstacles that are keeping you as a parent from engaging your kids with the impact of the principles in this chapter?

Before moving on from this moment, make a list of some simple next steps you can make now:

1)

2)

3)

Chapter 13

Statement #7 "I Love You!"

Other ways to say it: *"I care deeply for you."* / *"You mean so much to me."* / *"I choose you!"*/ *"I'm so grateful for you."*

The Need Being Met: Sensing, hearing, and receiving with assurance that we are cared for and wanted by those we value.

We should never assume others in our family know we love them. Our familiarity of living in such close association with our family members can lull us into thinking that our kids know this from us. Verbalize it—say these words!

Following Jesus' Words and Actions

I Love You. These three words strung together have been used in all kinds of settings, from movies, romance novels, secular songs, or to the craving for a certain dessert at your favorite restaurant. We are immersed in a world in which the meaning of the phrase, "I love you," has been hijacked and cheapened of its rich beauty by a world that doesn't grasp the heart of this expression. Saying "I love you" can speak life into the core of an individual's heart and confirm that they are treasured and cherished.

Let's take a fresh look at Jesus' actions of love for us. He not only is the author of love, but He is also the essence of love (1 John 4:8). He completely modeled every portion that conveys the full weight at the heart of what love is. He didn't just sit in Heaven when we were in such desperation and in need of rescue from our sin. He held nothing back from us and left where He was to come to us. He lived a sinless life, died on the cross, and rose again. He loved us, continues to love us, and will love us for eternity.

He has no limits to His love.

> [Love] bears all things, believes all things, hopes all things, endures all things. Love never ends (1 Corinthians 13:7–8a).

He showed us.

> God shows his love for us in that while we were yet sinners Christ died for us (Romans 5:8, RSV).

He was moved by obedience to His Father and His love for us. May we do the same as we love our kids and family; act and move in our love for them and say the words "I love you" to them. Once again, the relationship we have with our kids speaks volumes into the credibility that our kids give to our words, especially these three words. Following Jesus' modeling of His love for us, may our love for our kids be tethered to the quality of time we spend WITH them.

Saying Your Child's Name

Isn't it amazing—we can be in a crowded room with so many conversations happening and words being vocalized by so many people, but if someone says our name, it quickens our heart and grabs our attention immediately? When we hear our name, we are apt to lean in and look with expectancy. Our eyes and ears turn toward, and we listen. Using someone's name can cause that individual to pause for just a moment from other distractions and focus in, like a laser, to what you are about to say. Saying someone's name is a key to their heart.

Taking this reality into consideration, let's grasp as parents the power of using our kids' name followed with the phrase, "I love you!" Verbally affirm the weight of care you have in your heart for your child and speak straight into the vaults of their heart. Seize the opportunity to grab and hold their attention, if only for a moment, away from all the messages that are coming at them from culture. You love them and you desire to speak straight into who they are. No longer will we assume they know or listen to the lie that our kids don't really need to hear it.

Verbally affirm the weight of care you have in your heart for your child and speak straight into the vaults of their heart.

Saying "I Love You" Is for All the Nations and Our Homes

In 2017, my wife and I had the opportunity to go to Asia to lead a Marriage Enrichment weekend for pastors and their wives. We had a few days with them as we led breakouts, went on adventures such as hiking and kayaking as couples, and spent a lot of time in one-on-one conversations with each couple. In one of the breakouts, we encouraged them as couples to share with each other some of the statements that are in this book. When I got to the statement "I Love You" and challenged the husbands to go first and say these words to their wives, complete silence and a thick cloud of discomfort filled the room. In fact, most husbands stared at me with a look that could kill. The contempt on their faces shouted, "Why are you making me do the most uncomfortable thing possible?" The wives, on the other hand, were smiling hopefully into their husband's faces with great expectancy waiting for these precious words.

My wife and I learned several things in that moment in a room on the other side of the world. In that culture and area of Asia, the words "I Love You" are not said much to each other, even in a marriage relationship. Intimacy with words has a limit, and those three words are off-limits. I also saw with my eyes the deprivation on the faces of the wives and a longing to hear these words spoken to them by their husbands. The need was real, whether they had ever heard the words or not. The anticipation on their faces was obvious. Yes, many of the men said it, even though it might have been the most uncomfortable moment in those marriages. But many chose not to say it—and my wife heard it later in the wife's breakout. Both men and women said the vulnerability they felt when saying "I love you" was significant. When it was the wives turn to say these three words to their husbands, most husbands received it well. Saying the words "I Love You" might have pushed the boundaries for both men and women in that culture, but hearing those words is for everyone, everywhere. The need is real, and it conveys a message that we all long to hear.

Kids need to hear it and sense it often!

Setting the Table for God to Work

Setting the Table for your family is putting things in place now to foster and encourage characteristics that you want to happen on down the road.

How might you consider Setting the Table for your family that gives shape to your family life and impacts your kids heart? How might your vision of family life prepare relational spaces that shows them, "I love you" or "I choose you!"? Maybe you are ready to change the atmosphere of your home and how your family relates with each other, maybe you don't have kids yet, or your kids are young. You may envision family life that might not exist yet. Creating moments that immerse your child in an experience where they receive the message, "I love you!" puts anchors down when the storms come in your kid's life for them to know they are loved, even when they don't feel loved.

For instance, you might want conversations to happen at a deeper level, so you build into your calendar times for shared experiences that cultivates a trust level between both of you. You let them choose what to do. If you have a daughter, you enter her world and ask about things that she is passionate about. You listen, learn, and ask questions to truly discover what is on her heart. If she likes to drink coffee, then go to the coolest coffee shop! Sit across from her and let her take the conversation wherever she wants to take it. If you have a son, enter his world and ask him what he wants to do. Usually with boys, conversations happen best when you are doing something physical while talking. This could be throwing a football together, kicking a soccer ball back and forth, or while he's trying to teach you how to ice skate and play hockey.

Experiential and personal moments can awaken a depth that strengthens the relationship and continues to deepen the intentionality of the routine and ordinary.

These moments of building a relationship are vital for both of you. Don't wait for them to just happen. This might be one of the biggest hindrances in making it happen—we only think about these moments instead of making them materialize. Take the lead and create a Setting that allows for openness. Experiential and personal moments can awaken a depth that strengthens the relationship and continues to deepen the intentionality of the routine and ordinary.

Five Important Elements for Setting the Table

Think about the dinner table as a picture of everyday moments in family life. Build an intentional landscape that allows your love for your child to be caught as well as taught.

1. **Build Vision**—Draw in your mind and heart a depiction of what your everyday family life could look like. What are the characteristics you want to be present? Dreaming is free—so go big on this one!
2. **Plan and Prepare**—Just like preparing a table for a family meal, think through all the elements your kids might love. What is the "place setting" you put on the table? (your kids' personality, talents, passions) What type of "food" does your kid like? (things they like to do, topics they are passionate about, do they like to explore, play outside, etc.)

3. **Invite**—Let them know that you want them to join you. This is not a demand or an expectation. The request is an invitation because you choose them and want them present with you.
4. **Welcome**—Can hospitality be applied to our parenting style? Absolutely! Be generous and kind. Let's love them and let them know you are glad for these moments.
5. **Pray**—And pray BIG! Be specific and patient as you pray. Allow time for relationships to strengthen and space for conversations to happen.

Counterfeits and Vulnerabilities

- False or diluted definition of love—Love is defined by a world that identifies its meaning with strong feelings, lust, or covetousness. From song lyrics, movie dialogue, novels, and friends' discourse, the richness of God's definition of love is not only pushed to the sidelined but seen as antiquated and obsolete.
- I'm only loved and accepted by what I do and by how well I perform—*school, athletics, extracurricular activities*. If we aren't careful and diligent, we can simply tie the times and moments we say "I Love" to when our kids accomplish a task or do something we deem worthy. Our love for our kids is not conditional, so our communication of love to them should not be conditional either. This is especially true in times of discipline, or they sense we are disappointed in their actions. Let them know your love for them is not tied to their actions and nothing will change that. Kids need to hear I love you when things are calm and normal more than when things are ramped up and emotions are high.

- As stated in other chapters, this need is real and doesn't go away. Make sure the family is the place this need is being met!

Let's make the home the place your kids know they are loved the most!

Uncovering the Next Layer

- What are the fresh perspectives or opportunities that come to your mind?
- Related to the need mentioned in this chapter, what are the counterfeit messages or vulnerabilities that are evident right now in your family and kids?
- If you were being honest, what are the top obstacles that are keeping you as a parent from engaging your kids with the impact of the principles in this chapter?

Before moving on from this moment, make a list of some simple next steps you can make now:

1)

2)

3)

Chapter 14

Statement #8 "Join Me in Reaching People With the Gospel!"

Other ways to say it: *"Let's go on a mission trip together." / "Let's prayer walk our neighborhood together." / "Let's plan a serving day during our next vacation! Which local ministry would you like to serve with?"*

The Need Being Met: They are chosen and invited to join an adventure and grand experience, to be part of something bigger than themselves, and understand a relationship with Christ as every person's greatest need.

Invited to the Nations and Across the Street

We have the opportunity to invite our children to join us on one of the great responsibilities that has been given to us as believers. To go, tell, and make disciples across the street, to your city, or to the nations is a call from the Creator of all. What an opportunity for a family to take these occasions to do this together! You talk about an incredible shared experience as a family to live the adventure—this is it. We have all the components: The Great Commission (Matthew 28:18–20), parents and kids serving with each other, new areas of trust, overcoming a bit of fear, purpose, being out of our comfort zone together, a little bit of risk, adventure, and strengthening of faith. This has the makings of a real-life adventure movie with eternal value!

Six Common Responses

1. This idea seems far-fetched.
2. I've never considered doing missions as family.
3. I have no idea where to start even if we wanted to do missions as family.
4. I believe missions work is the church's responsibility.
5. We don't have time as family, we're too busy.
6. Sounds intriguing—let's go!

Each of these responses would not be unusual to hear from many of our homes. You are not alone if you picked more than one. But hear me out on something I would like you to consider. I believe many times in the American church, families are waiting for all the trips and opportunities to GO with the gospel to come from the church alone. Most of us have been conditioned over the years of doing church to wait for the call from the church when it comes to being on mission. It's as though the home's only response to going on mission is navigated completely by the staff or leadership of the local church. Besides, don't we pay them to do it all anyway?

I fully believe the church is tasked to mobilize, equip, and send out believers of all ages. I have planned, trained teams, and taken hundreds of students and adults to lots of places on mission with the local church and will continue doing this as long as I'm on church staff. But I believe our parents can also lead and invite their children to go on their own. Yes, the church has a major role to challenge and encourage its members to go, whether individuals or in groups, by inspiring, training, and deploying. But what if we as parents thought differently when it comes to going?

Let's absolutely be all in and join the church's efforts in going on mission journeys and local missions' opportunities. But let's also be observant on how we can mobilize as a family on our own, looking for areas that might be unique to our family's passions and circles of influence. The Great Commission has already come to us personally. God has already given us "marching orders." This conviction should impact our family values, our calendars, and our family budget meetings.

Two Challenging Questions

1. Have we distinctly separated the church world and regular world in our lives?
2. What can we do to align these to be one worldview that we live by?

Whether intentionally or not, our lives might be divided in two when it comes to what our family does with the church and after we leave the church building. When we get back home, we can easily settle back into our routine and carry on with everything else in our lives. We wait for the church to tell us what to do with our faith and then we leave our regular world and step back into the church world where God is waiting on us. Maybe we even have the tendency to check the box of missions or service, so we feel better about doing things in the church world. But once we finish, we step back into the regular world and carry on with our lives with eyes down on what culture has told us is important instead of eyes up on Whose we are and what we get to be doing.

When we are growing in our faith personally, listening to the call of Deuteronomy 6:6 by getting God's Word in our heart, our choices and our priorities change. As we lean into the Word by allowing His Spirit to transform our hearts, the two separate views of how we see the role of family brought on by the church world and the regular world distinctions begin to vanish. Our regular world and church world are now viewed through the lens of a gospel world view in our hearts and minds. We get to a point that we don't have to think about it. The gospel is elevated and intersects all areas of our family's life and impacts the choices we make and the things we do as a family.

The gospel influence of our choices becomes an identity of who we are as parents, which in turn is impressed upon the hearts of our kids and overall family identity. What we pay attention to and how we spend our time, we are transformed. Our calendar priorities adjust to what He is calling us to do. The content of our conversation changes; we observe people's situations at restaurants differently, and casual walks become prayer walks in the neighborhood. How and where we spend money and even moments on our vacations are viewed in a different way because what we now value is different. We don't jump in and out of our regular world and church world mindset because everything is all gospel centric.

As a parent, you have the privilege of inviting your child to join you on this extravagant adventure. Go to your neighbors by holding a Vacation Bible School in your backyard or serving as a family with a local gospel-centered ministry. Incorporate prayer walking and some family serving into your next vacation destination. Go on overseas mission trips together. Know you and your family are invited into what God is doing around the world. Let's go!

Four Shared Values Are Elevated

When we get to the point of inviting our kids to join us to reach others with the gospel in our neighborhood, with a local ministry, or even to the nations, four values begin to stir in the hearts and identity of your family. The invitation itself from you to your child serves as a proclamation of what is important to you.

1. **Shared Objectives**—The purpose and vision of the family is set by the parents through inviting their kids to join. *We're all in!*
2. **Shared Experiences**—These common experiences of going together create core memories that shape family identity. *This is who we are!*
3. **Shared Risks**—Most times when we as parents invite our kids along, we like to be experts in that given field. In missional adventures, we follow the Lord together and become a cohort often taking unknown steps forward in the greatest story. We aren't governed by risk avoidance because we recognize the calling that is greater. *Let's go for it!*
4. **Shared Conversations**—Engaging as a family in shared risks creates mutual discussion points—focusing on fears, rewards, rising to the challenge, and obedience to the Great Commission. Conversations eventually become centered on forward thinking and steps that can be taken. *Let's look for what's next!*

As we vocally invite our kids along on this journey of reaching people with the gospel and live this out alongside them, key principles can begin to move in the hearts of your kids:

1. This models and teaches your kids through actions what you value as a family and it's not just a theory that stays only in a church setting.
2. Being on mission as a family develops a family uniqueness built on living out the truths and calling of Scripture. When you build into your family a mindset of reaching people with the gospel, it can serve as a marker and distinctive for your family. So many characteristics cascade off this distinctive that have implications for your kids' identity.
3. Being on mission creates shared experiences and builds powerful memories that give shape to stronger relationships within the family.
4. The statement "join me" from a parent is powerful. Your kids recognize that you picked them for this quest—and you all join Jesus together as a family in His great invitation and command.
5. Your family is developing a purpose of offensive strategy with the gospel and not just playing defense. Parents are leading their kids to the best of life and not stuck in being content that their kids are saying no to temptations.
6. Kids develop an appreciation of the cost of discipleship and missions. When you say yes to His commands, there are areas you have to say no to. You are leading them to understand that it's worth it!
7. Going missionally changes how your kids see their friends, their school, and what they are learning through a gospel-

centric worldview. They begin to perceive spiritual aspects to varied experiences across their life.

8. Conversations change regarding what they talk about with you.
9. Family members are awakened to significance and greater purpose that we can all give our life to! This need is real and doesn't go away. Make sure the family is a place where this need is being met!
10. Prayer life changes. You and your family begin to pray differently and notice people around you with spiritual eyes. You begin to share a burden together for those who don't know Christ.

The statement "join me" from a parent is powerful. Your kids recognize that you picked them for this quest—and you all join Jesus together as a family in His great invitation and command.

Counterfeits and Vulnerabilities

1. *Church world and Regular world* differences may be evident in your family. Kids take notice when we shed the Church world wardrobe and get back to our everyday lives that make no mention of being on mission and living out the Great Commission.
2. We act as though missions or telling people about Jesus is something other people do. We will pay "professional" Christians to go.

3. We tend to adapt Jesus into our lives instead of listening and obeying His call and adapt our lives to Him. We can over-focus on sports, school, lifestyle, or career and often don't champion the eternal things of Scripture. We give lip service to the things of God.
4. One of the outcomes when our overall parenting mindset is not focused on advancing the gospel, our measurements of successful parenting can be skewed. We find ourselves celebrating the moments that our kids don't sin like their friends instead of furthering the message of hope in the gospel. Let's encourage, inspire, empower, and lead our kids toward missional living by going ahead of them and inviting them to join!

Let's make the home the place your kids are invited to be on mission the most!

Uncovering the Next Layer

- What are the fresh perspectives or opportunities that come to your mind?
- Related to the need mentioned in this chapter, what are the counterfeit messages or vulnerabilities that are evident right now in your family and kids?
- If you were being honest, what are the top obstacles that are keeping you as a parent from engaging your kids with the impact of the principles in this chapter?

Before moving on from this moment, make a list of some simple next steps you can make now:

1)

2)

3)

Chapter 15

That's How He Does It!

The Aha Moment of God's Handiwork in an Apple Orchard

Years ago, my extended family had set a week on the calendar to spend time together in the summer. We stayed in a cabin in the beautiful mountains of east Tennessee. Weeks like this with our whole family became important to us all, especially as our kids and all their cousins had become such a close group of friends. Our daughters and all their cousins were between three and ten, so we had plenty of energy in that vacation home. One of the nights for dinner, all 24 of us loaded up our cars and headed to a local restaurant favorite situated right next to a large apple orchard. While we were waiting for our tables, we stayed outside for the kids to run and play before sitting down at the tables. Suddenly, my four-year-old nephew came running out of the apple orchard he had been playing in. Our immediate reaction was that he had been stung or saw a snake among the trees. As he ran toward his mom, he pointed excitedly back at the rows of apple trees and yelled with enthusiasm, "Mom! That's how the Lord makes apples!"

What an aha moment he found himself in! He had never thought of the origin of apples, but he now had this flash of discovery! His face lit up with excitement and a physical eagerness burst forth to tell his

Family—that's how the Lord makes disciples!

mom. That's how God does it! When He shows us something new, built on what we have already taken in about Him, a sense of discovery erupts that causes us to want to shout.

This is my hope for you as you become encouraged with seeing family differently, maybe in a whole new way. Family—that's how the Lord makes disciples! This is His plan to carry His message to the next generation. These moments create in us a unique perspective of how we view the "why" of family.

Let's press on together!

The Significance of Nets Dropping and Doors Closing

> As he was walking along the Sea of Galilee, he saw two brothers, Simon (who is called Peter), and his brother Andrew. They were casting a net into the sea—for they were fishermen. "Follow me," he told them, "and I will make you fish for people." Immediately they left their nets and followed him (Matthew 4:18–20).

> After this, Jesus went out and saw a tax collector named Levi sitting at the tax office, and he said to him, "Follow me." So, leaving everything behind, he got up and began to follow him (Luke 5:27–28).

The descriptions in the Bible surrounding the actual moments when the early disciples were called to follow Jesus have always captivated me. Not only the privileged invitation given by Jesus to personally follow Him into the unknown, but the faith they stepped into by stepping out of everything they did know. The sound of fishing nets dropping on the ground tells the story of a tight grip that has now let go. The (possible) door closing as one leaves his tax office echoes a profound decision made to leave behind a sense of control.

Jesus beckoned to Simon and Andrew to follow Him, and they left their nets on the shore of the Sea of Galilee. Jesus called and Matthew literally stepped away from his tax office. But their responses reveal more than just a physical action. The nets and the booth represent what they knew and found security in, illustrating their career that enabled a lifestyle that led to where they found identity. They let go of a limited understanding of those three things, to follow the One who transforms how we view everything.

These new steps fashion a new well-worn path of spiritual influence of impressing God's Word onto the hearts of our kids in the mystery of the ordinary.

Whenever God challenges us to move and "drop our nets" or "get up from our office," He is calling us forward to walk in the Way—a way of life that is different. And this shapes how we live life with family. We leave old ways behind. Those current patterns that are ruts in the rhythms of family life, we must pop up out of them to make room for the new rhythms.

What are the nets you are gripping tight that you must let go of?

What is the booth you need to get up from and leave behind?

As we parent, we accept the challenge to make choices for creating new paths. These new steps fashion a new well-worn path of spiritual influence of impressing God's Word onto the hearts of our kids in the mystery of the ordinary. We step out in faith toward a new path of…

…a deeper walk with the Creator of all. Chisel God's Word in your heart, not just your mind.

…a release of my specific expectations I have for my kids' future and allow God to lead.

…a release of finding identity in my career and lifestyle and discover it in Christ.

…an embrace of the freedom found in Christ.

…the adventure of following the Lord's design of family that is like none other.

…carving out more time and availability with my kids by cutting away the non-essential items on my calendar.

…leaning into God's grace, mercy, and forgiveness as I'm honest with my own mess.

…seeking reconciliation with my kids if we find ourselves distant in our relationship because of one of our actions.

…a desire to recognize the content of my conversations and make the words I choose to speak to my kids well-thought-out and carefully considered.

…an awareness of the primary obstacles of family discipleship I might have discovered and give those over to God for His guidance and strength.

…a diligence in being awake to how God wants me to lead our family and children.

…not only a belief in building a relationship with my kids but making it a top value.

…a confidence in the influence of the ordinary in everyday life. Remember, "The place you find yourself as family, start there!" I'm excited for you on this journey!

Turn Toward You

(A Liturgy for Parents by JoEllen Taylor)

Father, from the beginning you created the family, the home as a reflection here of heavenly truths about belonging, source, and ultimate destination. Bound throughout by love, home is a crucible of formation and the cocoon for this life's longest relationships. What a gift as parents to steward such an idea!

We long to honor you well with this stewardship, for which we feel most unprepared, inadequate, and ill-equipped. Help us to trust Your keeping of all tender moments within and between us. Wrap your grace around the words we speak and clear our minds to perceive deeper needs.

Somehow the earthiness and common bodily things Jesus lived out comfort and encourage us as we care for the bodies and shepherd the souls of the children you entrust to us. You know from experience—whether as Creator, Father, or Son, all we feel and face in family.

Help us to welcome wilderness times in trust, feast with joy and laughter, and embrace opportunities of daily in and out, governed by the assurance that you are leading each one of us with love and purpose.

Knit us together for your glory. May we cheer one another on to follow You with abandon.

We need courage, Lord, to train in Scripture along the way, to sing of your goodness together, and to speak your name often. How unlike the world a life like this looks!

Expose our affection for the world to us as we sit with You, that we may turn our faces and lead our families toward true Light and away from counterfeit satisfaction and distraction.

You see the future for our children we so long to perceive. Help us allow space for You to develop them. Align us with you and use our home as a launching pad.

We long to claim their devotion that should rightly come second to their devotion for You. Keep before us the priority of giving You glory. Nudge us mercifully when we assume agency that truly belongs to You. Weave our surrendered parenting into the unfolding of Your work in them.

We confess our struggle to choose differently than our culture would dictate in priorities and practice. Help us choose daily dialog with eternity always in mind, knowing most of what we admire, and touch, offers only temporary pleasure and cannot support the weight of life's journey. As we enjoy sport, recreation, and rest, let us do so as worship of You, giver of all.

Help our wandering, cluttered minds to rest on You, turn toward You.

We will recall Your faithfulness and repeat to each other all the ways Your sustained care goes before and surrounds us. May Sabbath be a refreshing pattern in our families, Father! Thank you for teaching us Sabbath, as it rebukes our pretention of limitlessness.

We bless You, O Lord! Thank you for choosing us to walk in the way of family, designed and empowered by You to steward humanity. Help us to daily welcome the olive shoots You have placed around our tables, pliable, green, hungry, and thirsty, though they are. May we perceive the true and deeper hungers and thirsts around our family table and shepherd one another to You for deepest satisfaction.

Help us perceive the fruitfulness You are bringing about in this generation, and in those to come. May our tables be a place of blessing, sending, weeping, and joy, after Your heart. Find us ready to respond to You, Lord!

One day, free of the constraints of time, may our family, when all generations are gathered to You around Your table, lift our glasses in joyful agreement, testifying together to Your faithfulness forever!

Small Group Experience

These principles and the need to speak intentionally into our kids apply to all parental influencers. I believe you will be both encouraged and inspired to press forward, regardless of your family season, because we are looking beneath the surface to the ways family is designed by God to meet needs we all have. The target audience is parents of kids from preschool to high school, but the opportunity to influence grandparents, guardians, fostering parents, aunts and uncles, and even teachers and ministers is open.

Applicable to all make-ups of family—Every family is different due to factors like personality types, the family of origin of each parent, socio economic factors, ages, temperaments, depth of commitment to the Lord, extracurricular choices, parents in the home or not, athletic or not, academic or not, closeness of relationships (and many more factors) all play into the family dynamic and relationships. The heart of the 8 Statements all can be communicated in countless and creative ways within each of these family dynamics.

Applicable to all levels of spiritual maturity—From a seminary professor to a brand-new believer who has just picked up the Bible for the first time, the impact of intentional words in our families is practical for all.

For the group leader—As you prepare for each session, review the chapters covered in that session, and any Scripture passages referred to in the chapters. Mark anything you would like to make sure and highlight during the discussion, as well as any responses to questions you might share with the group. You will need a whiteboard or other way to do some group work.

Session 1—Chapters 1–3

- Give the group a moment to flip back through the chapters and assessment. Pray, asking God to guide the discussion and uncover what He wants to for each person in attendance.
- Begin by asking the group to picture one of their parents or other influential adults from their growing up years. Ask the group to share some characteristics or memories about them. Are the majority of the memories, stories, and qualities built from ordinary days or from extraordinary experiences? Much of the impact we have happens in the ordinary.
- From your book, share one or two of your own responses from chapters 1–3 of the book, and response questions to get the conversation started. The purpose of the assessment is reflection and to refer to personally, but if you feel comfortable, invite group members to share as they want to from their assessment responses and thoughts.
- Turn to the three circles graphic in chapter 3. Discuss any observations about what it takes to arrive at the place of greatest impact.
- What is one thing God has shown you about where your family is now?
- What things are you praying through?
- What next steps have you identified? For example, every week, spend one-on-one time with each of your children. No matter

their age. Go on "dates" with them and ask questions and then listen, take them on errands, invite them into your world.

- Arrange the class in groups of four to five to pray for one another.

Session 2—Chapters 4–6

- Give the group a moment to flip back through the chapters and assessment. Pray, asking God to guide the discussion and uncover what He wants to for each person in attendance.
- Invite group members to share responses and things they are processing from chapters 4–6.
- From your book, share some of your own responses from chapters 4–6 of the book, and response questions at the end of each chapter.
- On the whiteboard, make two columns—Wants and Needs. As a group, make a comprehensive list together of wants and needs of the kids represented in the room. When the lists are built out, ask, "how much time are we spending speaking to the wants of our kids, and how much to the needs?"
- What are some ways we can become more aware of the deeper needs of our kids?
- What is one thing God has shown you about your child in the last few weeks?
- What things are you praying through?
- What next steps have you identified?
- Arrange the class in groups of four to five to pray for one another.

Session 3—Chapters 7–9

- Give the group a moment to flip back through the chapters. Pray, asking God to guide the discussion and uncover what He wants to for each person in attendance.
- Open the discussion on chapters 7–9 of the book, and response questions at the end of each chapter, inviting the group to share any responses they would like to. Be willing to share from your journaling or prayer responses.
- What is God stirring in your own heart as you reflect on the importance of belonging, knowing you are prayed for, and knowing you are believed in?
- Ask a group member to list on the whiteboard as many times and ways to pray as possible for your child and let them know you are praying.
- What is one deeper need you have become aware of in your child?
- What are you giving thanks for in your family this week?
- How are you talking with your kids in new ways?
- Arrange the class in groups of four to five to pray for one another.

Session 4—Chapters 10–12

- Give the group a moment to flip back through the chapters. Pray, asking God to guide the discussion and uncover what He wants to for each person in attendance.
- Open the discussion on chapters 10–12 of the book, and response questions at the end of each chapter, inviting the group to share any observations or responses they would

like to. Be willing to share from your journaling or prayer responses.

- The three statements we are discussing this week are big and deep. Faith talks, walking through hard days with our kids, and dealing with forgiveness require wisdom. How can we be alert to moments God opens for us to speak into these things?
- Brainstorm together as many ways as possible to authentically speak about Jesus or bring Scripture into your daily conversation. If someone shares that it feels awkward, talk about that as a group. Why does it? What can we do to overcome this obstacle?
- What are some ways creation gives us opportunities to talk about God with our kids?
- What are you giving thanks for in your family this week?
- Arrange the class in groups of four to five to pray for one another.

Session 5—Chapters 13–15

- Give the group a moment to flip back through the chapters. Pray, asking God to guide the discussion and uncover what He wants to for each person in attendance.
- Open the discussion on chapters 13–15 of the book, and response questions at the end of each chapter, inviting the group to share any observations or responses they would like to. Be willing to share from your journaling or prayer responses.
- Share some fresh ways you have been able to say, "I love you" to your kids recently.

- On the whiteboard, list together some ways your family can go on mission in the ordinary, and in the extraordinary days—locally, regionally, or internationally.
- Close out your time together as a group by celebrating some things God has done in your family during the weeks you've spent in this study. Share specific times you have spoken into your child's life in new ways no matter what their immediate response is. Finish by reading "Turn Toward You"—a liturgy for parents.